Lighten Up and Log In for Love

Lighten Up and Log In for Love

■ ■ ■

How Humor Helps Baby Boomers Survive Online Dating

Eric Robespierre

ISBN-13: 9780692909928
ISBN-10: 0692909923
Library of Congress Control Number: 2017911548
CreateSpace Independent Publishing Platform
North Charleston, South Carolina

Published by Eric Robespierre
www.ericrobespierre.com

Also by Eric Robespierre

The Yummy Hunter's Guide
The Best-Tasting, Low-Calorie Foods and Where to Shop for Them
(With Helen Brand)

Cracking the Walnut
How Being a Little Nuts Helped Me to Beat Prostate Cancer

Living Large in America
The Life and Times of the Family Ginsburg (pronounced Du Pont)

*Dedicated to all those of my generation
who bravely venture into the world of cyberspace
in search of love and romance.*

What sunshine is to flowers, smiles are to humanity.
These are but trifles, to be sure;
but scattered along life's pathway,
the good they do is inconceivable.

—Joseph Addison

Preface

Laughter is the shortest distance
between two people.

—Victor Borge

I can hear you saying, who is this Eric Robespierre character to lecture me on how to find love on a dating site? Has he ever cried, ever felt the anguish, the disappointment of online rejection? Has his frustration become so intolerable he almost tossed his MacBook Air out the window and really gave it, and online dating, the air?"

When I entered the world of online dating, I was in my midsixties. My girlfriend, who I had been with for the past five years, told me she needed some space. Previously, I had been married for nearly thirty years, and those two relationships were the sum of my dating experiences.

At the time I was writing a book with a woman who was a veteran of online dating, and she made a good case for me to join. My initial reaction was to refuse. I had read numerous online profiles and thought they were painfully unoriginal, unimaginably boastful, and made men of my generation sound, excuse my French, full of shit!

I finally relented when I told my friend I'd join if I could write a profile that best represented who I really was. I came up with a set of outrageous but tongue-in-cheek demands and welcomed any woman who could meet them. When my friend gave her approval, I took a chance and joined my first, and only, online dating site.

My profile drew rave reviews. Immediately, I began to receive numerous messages. I eventually corresponded with hundreds of women. Dated quite a few. Many became friends and confidants. I became privy to their stories of love and agony. Male friends also began sharing their experiences, recalled their successes and failures, and relayed their own cautionary tales.

I can say with great certainty—I know your pain. Let me say it again… *I know your pain!* The pain that comes from disappointment, disappointment that, amazing as it may be, the person you've finally met is not the person of your dreams but the screaming harridan of your nightmares!

How about the feelings of regret when, after hearing their sweet voice on the phone, you discover they recently bench-pressed five hundred pounds at Gold's Gym?

Or, if he wrote he was your age; he shows you a family album featuring a photo of him and Babe Ruth?

Oh right! She bragged about how thin she was, so how come she had to turn sideways to come through the door?

She swore over and over that she was a one-man gal, so how come she couldn't keep her eyes off every guy who came into Starbucks?

Speaking of Starbucks, have you ever seen anyone rip open ten packs of raw sugar with his or her teeth, suddenly pour them into his or her coffee because he or she says, "You need to put a little zing into your thing."

I can go on and on, but despite all the stories of angst you would think belong in *Ripley's Believe It or Not,* I came to the realization the words of Ella Wheeler Wilcox would serve as my guide to surviving the perils of online dating:

> *Laugh, and the world laughs with you;*
> *Weep, and you weep alone.*

To accomplish this, I came up with a personal list of *Dos and Don'ts* that immediately put a smile on my face; even forced a few giggles when dating got particularly difficult due to my own insecurities, lack of common sense, and overactive libido.

It is my desire that in sharing this list I'll be able to put the same smiles on your face, prompt you into a few guffaws as you take up the daunting task of first filling out your profile, then perusing those who make you want to jump up and sing "Sweet Sue," and finally—dealing with the messages of love and desire that fly back and forth from your heated inbox to theirs.

To help me accomplish this, I have enlisted a group of online vets to share their stories and e-mails and plucked pertinent postings I have personally received or spotted during my years of online dating to provide additional color, wisdom, and even more laughter.

Finally, I have included poetic sayings and movie quotes about love that should remind us never to lose sight of what's really at the heart of this book.

My advice, stories, and interviews are often over the top. Believe me, if I could have found another way to amuse you that did not resort to exaggeration, while at the same time limit my intake of Chianti Classico, I would have done it!

I leave you with the thought that laughter got me through the experience of online dating, with mind, body, and a sense of humor, still intact. Just as important, it left me with the impression that even at our tender age, love and romance is still possible for my fellow baby boomers.

■   ■   ■

Introduction

Look. It's simple.
Throw enough mud against the wall
and something will stick.

—Helen, fifties, divorced. (Online Veteran)

ABANDON HOPE, ALL ye who enter here. No, I'm not quoting from Dante's *Inferno;* I'm only repeating the mantra of a battle-scarred vet who eventually confessed the only thing that got her through the online dating scene was her nightly pint of ice cream.

Another weary traveler, also using a food analogy confided, "You have to break a few eggs to make an omelet."

Who would have thought they serve brunch in cyberspace? Is it any wonder baby boomers are popping Xanax instead of m&m's when one hears stories of such Sturm und Drang?

When I went online, the first thing my friends clued me in on was the *three-date rule.* They said, on the third date you're going to have sex. I'm still not certain if it was something I said or did, or if the whole idea was an urban legend; you know, like alligators in the sewers, but it's never worked out for me. Oh, make sure you don't call for a fourth date if, the night before, you stood outside her window yelling: You cow! Can't you count!

No, that wasn't me, no matter what anyone told you! I'm simply beginning this introductory section with a little humor, aimed particularly to those of you new to online dating who, I believe to be the most fearful of all. Not to worry, I've done the heavy lifting so, when you log in, you won't experience *psychic hernia.*

To those poor souls who've already suffered the heartbreak of online dating, I've got your back, too. Even if you're continuing to suffer panic attacks due to buyer's remorse (should have trusted your instincts and not joined a site for polygamists); have been intimidated by the slings and arrows of social ridicule (friends sold you out for their free subscription); or the most mortifying of all (your child posted an unauthorized version leaving you with thoughts of killing them at Thanksgiving); this is what I have to say to you...*it's time to get some sugar...sugar.*

If you've been on multiple dating sites, you know each one creates its own method of presenting your profile, using their own specific terminology. There is no way I can duplicate this variety, however, all share four basic elements; and if I can show you how to successfully navigate them, you can travel through all sites without a hitch.

They are: The Photo, The Essay, The Yes/No/Check Here Sections, and The Short-Answer Questionnaire.

I address them in the sequence they usually occur, so simply follow my suggestions, and you'll be able to extrapolate your own answers to fit any variation. This does not mean trying to figure out what they want to hear and then giving it to them. (Like when did that ever work out for you, right?)

A word to veterans of online dating: I'm not asking you to change previous strategies or totally reinvent yourself; just keep an open mind and see how you may be able to incorporate my suggestions to make your profile even better.

To you newbies, regardless of how elementary (stupid, idiotic) these sections appear, unless you pay strict attention to my *dos and don'ts,* you'll let your guard down (as I almost did) and come up with answers that make you appear equally moronic

Pay close attention, and you'll never have to pick up your phone and hear a voice so unintelligible; you actually believe they're talking with a handful of marbles in their mouth.

Listen and learn; visions of running your hands through a full head of luxurious silver hair won't be shattered when, at your first meeting, you peer over your double cappuccino and wonder *how he could have gone bald overnight.*

Pursue my advice diligently and avoid dinner with a woman who chose the restaurant because it's where her ex-spouse confessed to an affair with her best friend, and then went into detail about how she tried to kill him over dessert.

Lastly, follow my *dos and don'ts,* and you will never receive an e-mail written by someone learning to spell—in a language, even Google Translate can't decipher.

OK—perhaps I'm again being too flippant and exaggerating just a mite—remember—it's all for the greater good. *If hyperbole is the music of love, play on!*

■　■　■

Think of it as an all-you-can-eat buffet where you can fill up to your heart's content without gaining a pound, growing an inch, or throwing up afterward.
FC, fifty-nine, divorced

■　■　■

What is that great line from Forrest Gump about life is a box of chocolates; never know what you're getting? Well, that's the way I looked at this Internet thing.
Nan, fifty-nine, divorced

■　■　■

I wasn't going to let my kids tell me I wasn't with it. Like they invented sex, drugs, and rock and roll? Nobody's going to start a revolution without me!
Jack, fifty-nine, widower

■　■　■

What made me finally choose the Internet was when I thought it had gained nationwide attention and it wasn't so selective. I felt safer, thought I'd find more people like me, you know normal. Gay, straight, whatever, the best thing since I discovered the Brioche!
SA, fifties, single

■   ■   ■

You want to know my approach to all this Internet dating? Just be honest. Be yourself, and if he thinks you're awesome…and you think the same of him… gangbusters! If he doesn't, it's his loss. Works for me.
Chris, sixty-seven, divorced

■   ■   ■

I don't know who told you about a "third-date rule," but the guys I seem to meet ask for sex even before the waiters take our drink orders. These are guys who write in their profile they want companionship, long-lasting relationships, and maybe marriage. What a crock. It's the Viagra talking. Some even take it out and show me the dosage. Don't get me wrong, I'm not complaining.
Helen, fifties, divorced

■   ■   ■

Make Dun & Bradstreet your friend. One guy told me he owned ten franchises of a certain fast-food chain. Liar! Another told me he was in the construction business and responsible for two famous towers in the Phoenix area. Big liar! The last one tried to sweet-talk me by telling me he had his own Caribbean Island and for our first date, was going to fly me there, on his private jet. Really big liar!
CP, fifties, divorced

■   ■   ■

Choosing a Site

■ ■ ■

Who so loves believes the impossible.

—Elizabeth Barrett Browning

I TOLD YOU it was a friend who convinced me to join online dating. She was also the one to suggest a certain site she had success with, one she argued, would bring me equal good fortune.

Call it luck, I had only good experiences, but in your case, let's not leave anything to chance. Let's make sure you'll only have good fortune on your side.

■ ■ ■

Do: Forget the axiom *Man plans, and God laughs* when joining a religious site.

■ ■ ■

Do: Select hookup sites if you love spy novels and perfected the art of following people using your GPS.

■ ■ ■

Do: Join a political site, because you liked the actors from *The West Wing*. Birds of a feather do flock together.

■ ■ ■

1

Do: Chose one that attracts like-minded individuals who, like you, have to be institutionalized during Halloween.

■ ■ ■

Don't: Use a Ouija board again. Once burned, twice warned, remember?

■ ■ ■

Don't: Pick it if you have to use Google Translate to read the name.

■ ■ ■

Don't: Think about religious sites, unless you're ready to change your meal plan.

■ ■ ■

Don't: Disregard senior sites, because your hairdresser said you look like your daughter.

■ ■ ■

Don't: Join a site, because it's where your girlfriend got her dreamboat. Remember pyramid schemes—first in, first out.

■ ■ ■

Absolutely Do Not: Think Photoshop and wearing disguises will fool anybody, unless you subscribe to the theory, *love is blind*.

■ ■ ■

I loved their commercials, and the people who got together looked like me.
Linda, sixties, widow

■　■　■

I don't go to church, but there is something about the religious sites that make me feel all warm and safe.
Leslie, sixties, divorced

■　■　■

I liked sites that ask you to fill out lots of questions. I figured any man who takes the trouble to answer them was as serious as me about finding a long-term relationship. I mean, that's just obvious, isn't it?
KK, late fifties, widow

■　■　■

I looked at Match but didn't like because it was someone just looking at photos saying, "OK, let's go out and have drinks." I have girlfriends who want that. For them, "Happy Hour" is where it's at. I wanted something with more substance. Call me old fashioned.
Hank, sixty, widower

■　■　■

I can't believe my friends are on multiple sites. They say they're covering all the bases. How do you keep track of each one? I'm only on the one, and sometimes I lose track of what I've posted. Not them. They print out each profile, file 'em in folders, and know exactly where what is where. True, I'm telling you the truth.
C, sixty-nine, widow

■　■　■

I thought I'd try one of those sites that hook you up with people in real time. That way, if I saw somebody I liked on the street or at the market, all I had to do was swipe his picture; if he did the same, we'd meet. My girlfriend, Meryl, is always on it. Unfortunately, one day, she ran right into a lamppost, needed five stitches in her head so...I was a bit apprehensive, only used it at Fairway. They have big aisles. I didn't have much success, but while I was huddled behind the apples, a guy asked if I needed some help. One thing led to another, you know how that goes? We went out for coffee. Nice guy, possibilities...seeing him for dinner this weekend.

Donna, sixty-eight, divorced

■ ■ ■

Selecting Parameters

■ ■ ■

Love isn't something you find.
Love is something that finds you.

—LORETTA YOUNG

THIS IS GOING to be one of your most frustrating sections, because as a woman friend confided: *They just want what they want, when they want it.*

Nevertheless, if you only prefer gentlemen who reside within certain limits, you must stick to your guns and don't waver. Do not stray out of your zip code, and for heaven sake, don't call a moving company to get an estimate on what it would cost to move from your big city condo to a ranch in the foothills of Montana. *So he was the only one to contact you! Don't panic!*

Guys—don't think this cautionary tale doesn't apply to you. Don't let your sex drive drive you out of your rent-stabilized apartment. When your libido starts cashing checks your brain can't cover, you'll find yourself paying market rate.

On the flip side, if you're outside their parameters, you can't play games like that either.

Don't think I wasn't tempted. I was one click away from contacting an extremely alluring woman living in Cape Breton, who set her sights on men from Halifax. What possessed me to think I'd ever seriously relocate to Nova Scotia when I won't even cross the Hudson to meet a woman in Jersey? (Come on, she was gorgeous!)

A cold shower and an equally provocative profile of a lady from the Upper West Side quickly returned me to my senses.

5

I have broached the relocation topic with several online vets who adamantly denied being so desperate as to ever contemplate doing such a foolhardy thing; nevertheless, I swear, I detected a twinkle of recognition in their eyes as we talked.

■ ■ ■

Do: Realize parameters don't count if they live in a *motor home.*

■ ■ ■

Do: Recognize *From Sea to Shining Sea* doesn't mean Malibu but the *Tortugas.*

■ ■ ■

Do: Realize the more you expand the miles, the more you increase your chances of paying their travel expenses.

■ ■ ■

Do: Understand, if you live in a prime location and choose within ten miles, enterprising daters will rent a hotel room.

■ ■ ■

Don't: Add...*wherever Latin lovers live* if you can't tango.

■ ■ ■

Don't: Show desperation and write, *Have Uber, will travel.*

■ ■ ■

Don't: Use kilometers. This is code for *I want a European with a title.*

■ ■ ■

Don't: Declare *all he needs is a GPS*, because you'll lose guys who love their maps.

■ ■ ■

Don't: Be surprised when you get pleas for visas and work permits when you write, *lovers without borders.*

■ ■ ■

Absolute Do Not: Be annoyed when you write *within city limits,* and he lives in another country. After all, how many guys do you know who follow directions?

■ ■ ■

The longer I went without a date, the further I expanded my parameters.
Gavin, seventy-two, widower

■ ■ ■

Sailed halfway around the world, and I am ready to sail to the other half with you.
GGG, sixty-five, widow

■ ■ ■

I put in one hundred miles, because I was relocating…I got guys from out of the country. Give 'em a mile, they give you an ocean. I made that up.
Laura, late sixties, widow

■ ■ ■

I'm from London, a long time ago. Would it be possible to find a partner who'd like to spend part of the year on both sides of the Pond—both London/UK and New York? A partner with whom to adventure, explore, travel, cycle, hike, and cook.
NCB, fifty-nine, divorced

■　■　■

I received an e-mail from a woman who spends five months a year in New York City, the rest of the time in Brazil. I thought this arrangement was not healthy for me, because I wanted someone full-time. Unfortunately, she was so attractive, so fascinating, I said yes to me meeting her. At the last minute, I canceled. My better instincts kicked in and saved me.
Steve, midsixties, widower

■　■　■

I have to admit I traveled out of my socioeconomic comfort zone several times— once to Princeton New Jersey, twice up to Greenwich Connecticut, and once just a few miles up First Avenue to Sutton Place. Each liaison was predictable had I been less egotistical, more clear-eyed, and just plain practical. No matter the physical or mental attraction, there was no way I could afford to live in their world, even if they were amenable to sharing expenses.
The Author

■　■　■

Picking Your Screen Name

■ ■ ■

What's in a name? That which we call a rose
By any other name would smell as sweet.

—WILLIAM SHAKESPEARE, *ROMEO AND JULIET*

WHEN I ASKED the woman who talked me into going online for her advice, she simply said: use your imagination; whatever you do, don't use your real name. Well, duh, I wasn't that naïve.

I thought my best approach was to see how other guys were promoting themselves, become inspired by their cleverness; certainly get a feel for what men thought would successfully grab a woman's attention.

MrBig, ThePileDriver, and *Mr24HrMan*, all with the obligatory *69s* affixed were taken, leaving me no choice but to brag about...my love of movies.

Not to draw a distinction between the sexes, but I have never seen such sexually charged female *noms de plume.* One male friend shared his disappointment, confiding that he'd sell his soul to meet a woman named *OverEasy.*

■ ■ ■

Do: Use *Cellophane* if you want to be absolutely transparent.

■ ■ ■

Do: Think screen names matter, because men will go to their graves for *ABodyToDieFor*.

■ ■ ■

Do: Decide on *ComeHither if you want a guy who takes directions.* (Good luck on that one!)

■ ■ ■

Do: Look at the name on your AARP card before you choose high-school nicknames like *JuicyLucy or JackTheBoyWonder*.

■ ■ ■

Don't: State the obvious and call yourself *DirtyOldMan*.

■ ■ ■

Don't: Choose *Anonymous* and then add your name and number.

■ ■ ■

Don't: Call yourself *MrICanGoAllNight*, unless you have a death wish, or thinks she does.

■ ■ ■

Don't: Confuse delusion with illusion, and use the size of your hands or feet in the name.

■ ■ ■

Don't: Use *JackBeNimble,* unless you can unzip your fly in less than twenty seconds.

■ ■ ■

Don't: Call yourself *ClaudiaFromTheBlock* when you live on a farm and don't even have a zip code.

■ ■ ■

Don't: Select *TheBeautifulBlondeFromBashfulBend* or any location that can't be found on MapQuest.

■ ■ ■

Don't: Call yourself a *BodaciousSetOfTa'sta's.* He may not be familiar with Southern terms of endearment.

■ ■ ■

Don't: Use *ShopToYouDrop,* even though your shrink says the first step to getting better is to acknowledge your illness.

■ ■ ■

Don't: Be discouraged if the name has been taken; just add as many numbers after it until the site accepts *NobodyDoesItBetter.*

■ ■ ■

Don't: Go overboard. *EllynBlk* is OK; but *Ellyn711715thAve4B* is too much, unless you're looking for Larry Johnson, who lived upstairs.

■ ■ ■

Don't: Choose *YoungerThanSpringtime*, *PureAsThe DrivenSnow* or *Cold HandsWarmHeart*; most guys, can't handle two thoughts at once.

■ ■ ■

Absolutely Do Not: Choose any forms of *Happy*, like *Happy Face*, *Happy Lady*, or worst of all, *Always Happy*. Get real; he knows that won't happen the minute he takes control of the remote.

■ ■ ■

I'm Mr. Satisfaction! Mr. You've Got a Big Ego, is more like it.
Helen, fifties, divorced

■ ■ ■

My biggest problem…I had a hard time picking out a screen name. I don't know why. I didn't expect that would be the problem. I finally settled on BrownEyed Girl 10e. You know the song and my apartment number?
And how did that work out?
Very well. Lots of Van Morrison fans, and they're all cute, too.
GGG, sixty-five, widow

■ ■ ■

His screen name was DreamLoverBobby. I can see why. He posted pictures of himself when he was young, and I swear he's the spitting image of Bobby Darin. You're of the age you remember how all the girls loved Bobby D and that song. Obviously, this Bobby doesn't look like that now. He's a bit overweight, balding, not really physically appealing, but the screen name, and the way he looked when he was nineteen—well—I had to give him a try. It took me four dates, but he grew on me. I shouldn't say that, should I? Actually, the more we talked, did things together, the more attractive he became. And, no, every time I look

at him, I don't see Bobby Darin. I see Bobby, last name to remain anonymous, who I'm thoroughly happy with, and who's become my dream lover.
FC, fifty-nine, divorced

■　■　■

You want to know the craziest thing that ever happened to me on a dating site? Her screen name was "Sports Angel67." Talk about having game! In her essay she writes she's an interior designer known for decorating Man Caves to look like sports fields and arenas. I should have figured she was a nutcase, instead I thought cool; she was mixing her love of sports with her profession. Anyway, I contacted her, told her straight away I'm a Yankees' fan, and since she says she is too, pls—she's sixty-seven like me, hence the "67" in her name—we could reminisce about the good ole days. We agree to meet at Central Park South in front of what was the old Mickey Mantle's steakhouse. She has me standing out there for a half-hour, in the f-ing cold, telling me how she hung out at the bar for two straight months until Micky finally came in, and she could get him to sign her collection of Mickey Mantle's cards—that—she doesn't hesitate to say is now worth a goddamn fortune. She then looks at her watch, tells me she's got another appointment—I should give her a buzz, and walks off. My feet were two blocks of f-ing ice. What a crazy bitch!
Gavin, seventy-two, widower

■　■　■

Choosing the Best Subscription Plan

— ■ ■ ■ —

*Edward: You know what the difference is between a dream
and a goal?
He used to say to me. A plan.*

—JODI PICOULT, *LONE WOLF*

I WAS AGAIN lucky to have my author-friend help me to choose the right plan; otherwise, I might have followed the advice of Larry, my downstairs' neighbor, which would have sent me into *Subscription Interuptus* with the following:

"The secret, you always have to be fresh meat. Which translates into something new and entirely different. What could be more enticing than an Irishmen going onto a site for Philippines? Another secret—only go for trial subscriptions, stay on 'em for a week, then you're gone."

I recently met up with him, and despite the fact he had been banned from every ethnic site imaginable, he thought the underlying idea is still workable and was getting ready to visit ethnic bars around the boroughs.

We all have someone like Larry whispering in our ear. My advice, don't listen. Just read on.

■　■　■

Don't: Be a sore loser and give up after the trial period.

■　■　■

Don't: Choose it because you can add miles on your Amex.

■ ■ ■

Don't: Be a buzzkill, and automatically select *Automatic Renewal*.

■ ■ ■

Don't: Choose *trial period* because you're too cheap to buy more Viagra.

■ ■ ■

Don't: Think you'll get your money back if you claim the site made you love sick.

■ ■ ■

Don't: Use Google Translate because you think the language of love is universal.

■ ■ ■

Don't: Game the system by opening accounts under different names to extend the trial period.

■ ■ ■

Don't: Be *penny wise and pound-foolish* and pick it because you have eighteen months to pay it off.

■ ■ ■

Don't: Be so full of yourself and only consider the trial-period option. When is the last time your barber ever told you the truth?

■ ■ ■

Don't: Select it because joining with a friend gets you 50 percent off. Remember, *Man plans, God laughs*; they'll probably steal your date.

■ ■ ■

Absolutely Do Not: Forget my reference to *Man plans, and God laughs* when one of the choices on a religious site is—*Leave It in His Hands.*

■ ■ ■

I'm having a difficult and confusing time with the dating site system. I may never be able to connect w u again; it's like the "Matrix" to me.
Nan, fifty-nine, divorced

■ ■ ■

I always choose to belong to two sites at a time. One religious, well it's really more a cultural thing; the second, something more open, not something kinky, if you know what I mean? I change up the pictures and use different screen names. Sometimes I get them mixed up but only in a fun way.
Helen, fifties, divorced.

■ ■ ■

Honestly, don't recall why I picked three months. That first day seems so far removed. What does stand out is the last day and how I received an e-mail I almost didn't read, because, honestly, I had given up. Been dating now for almost three months. How's that for a love story?
Linda, sixties, widow

■ ■ ■

My subscription on Match ends this October. After ten years on and off various sites in an attempt to find the last great love of my life, finally decided to take an extended break. How long? Not sure I even know. Oh, not giving up on dating. I'll go to "Happy Hour." I might even go on a fix-up. I forgot, you wanted to know about my experiences online. You can imagine, in ten years there's been a lot of men I've fallen in and out of love with…no, wait. I'm becoming too melancholy, and I want you to turn off the tape recorder.
GGG, sixty-five, widow

■ ■ ■

The Photo

■ ■ ■

You have bewitched me body and soul,
and I love, I love, I LOVE YOU.

—JANE AUSTEN, *PRIDE AND PREJUDICE*

BLAME IT ON our DNA, but the three most important things to a man when he looks over your profile are—your looks, your looks, and your looks. Therefore, the first *do* is to make certain your picture(s) charms, captivates, and finally captures the poor fool, so that he either contacts you right there on the spot or is so intrigued, he continues reading without so much as taking a breath between sentences.

Lose him here, and you lose him forever. This does not mean going to DEFON 5 and posting someone else's photo, no matter how closely you think you resemble Charlie Sheen or Charlize Theron.

I know, I know, your hairdresser swears up and down you look like her. Well, my barber tells me I look like Richard Gere. It's a *confederacy of duplicity,* designed at getting more tips. (Damn it, if it doesn't work!)

So, before you think this kind of outrageous substitution is a good idea, let me warn you, unless he shows up blindfolded (will talk kinky later), is blind (don't kid yourself, sightless men fib, too)—you'll certainly attract a like-minded suitor, most probably an Elvis impersonator!

(*Warning! Don't blame yourself if the most primitive of my species refuses to read the rest of your profile, because he doesn't like your photo. This type of primordial behavior is beyond your control. Besides, you don't want a Mr. Neanderthal for a partner. If you do, close my book and post that photo of Charlize.*)

(Hold it! Going to do something I may later regret, but I'm calling out the guy, and you know who I mean, that posts a photo of George Clooney! How's that been for you—you loser!)

■   ■   ■

Do: Make natural light your friend. You're on a dating site, not in a *National Geographic* special featuring nocturnal cave animals.

■   ■   ■

Do: Find someone who knows how to work a camera. Nobody looks their best when caught red-face, screaming: *"Wait for the f'ing red light to go on!"*

■   ■   ■

Don't: Stand with a group. This isn't a guessing game!

■   ■   ■

Don't: Take pics during your stress test to prove you're in good shape.

■   ■   ■

Don't: Hide your face in shadows. What—you're on the *FBI's most wanted list?*

■   ■   ■

Don't: Include children unless you want to look like an old fogey or cradle robber.

■   ■   ■

Don't: Pose in a Speedo, unless you're prepared to mention your addiction to steroids.

■   ■   ■

Don't: Sit on anyone's lap. This isn't a Christmas photo, and the letch you're posing with isn't Santa.

■   ■   ■

Don't: Use Photoshop and become *the new you,* because they won't recognize *the real you* when you show up on a date.

■   ■   ■

Don't: Sit in a photo booth. Two steps up from a mug shot, and you always end sticking your tongue out and looking stupid.

■   ■   ■

Don't: Take selfies, unless you think magnifying moles, food caught in your teeth, or enlarging your nose tenfold is attractive.

■   ■   ■

Don't: Pose wearing gold letters hanging from your neck spelling out your name. This is a dating site, not a police booking.

■   ■   ■

Don't: Try to look taller. Nothing makes your features more grotesque than having the photographer lie on the ground while you look down at the camera.

■   ■   ■

Don't: Go for Botox the night before. Forget trying to smile—what about looking like *rigor mortis has set in*? (Guys—I'm talking to you, too.)

■　■　■

Don't: Use Photoshop. This second warning is directed at the color-blind or anyone who thinks magenta is on a skin-tone chart.

■　■　■

Don't: Pose with animals, unless you want to play second fiddle to a dolled-up French poodle or scare off women who don't like pythons.

■　■　■

Don't: Take pictures in a national park. I don't care how tall you are; even Wilt Chamberlain looks like a midget when standing in front of a sequoia.

■　■　■

Don't: Post teenage pics. Nothing is more pathetic than the viewer lamenting how somebody so young and good-looking could turn into—*you*.

■　■　■

Don't: Take photos in outfits you wouldn't wear to Thanksgiving dinner. Might want to save looking like Lolita or a dominatrix, until the second date.

■　■　■

Don't: Ask strangers to take photos. Nothing ruins the picture more than running after someone who has just stolen your iPhone 7.

■　■　■

Don't: Mess with the camera. Can't make a silk purse out of a sow's ear; no soft focus, Vaseline gauze, or other kinds of exotic filtrations.

■   ■   ■

Don't: Substitute emojis for your smiley face. This isn't a dating site for stick figures, even though some dates turn up undernourished or as cartoonish.

■   ■   ■

Absolutely Do Not: Keep your picture blank! Does *Playboy and Playgirl* blank out their centerfold? I rest my case!

■   ■   ■

If I see another guy baring his naked chest and making a muscle, I'm going to vomit.
Ellyn, late fifties, divorced

■   ■   ■

He had this photo of him standing next to his fancy new Mercedes that had tinted windows. You know, only men who have something to hide have them, so you bet, I reported him to the site.
FC, fifty-nine, divorced

■   ■   ■

I don't like to see stupid captions like, "This is me and my son celebrating my birthday at the top of Mt. Fuji." You don't see guys writing, "this is me and my pal Larry puking our guts out against the wall at the Beach Tavern."
NCB, fifty-nine, divorced

■   ■   ■

Post pictures of you at a wedding? You want me to tell you about posting wedding pictures? Any guy with a brain knows you've spent the whole day at beauty parlor, probably spent a fortune on a dress, spent the last six months starving yourself to lose weight, all goes downhill from there.
Helen, fifties, divorced

■ ■ ■

My boyfriend's name is Bobby, and what got me was how cool he looked in his white blazer and black cowboy hat. E-mailed him, said I liked his "chapeau." Met for coffee, been together ever since. Took me a year, but it was worth it.
Linda, sixties, widow

■ ■ ■

I know immediately if his profile picture has him sitting behind a desk, he's going to weigh two hundred pounds. Odds come down to fifty-fifty if it's just a facial shot. Not much you can do, just hope for the best. Me? Full-figured photo. What you see is what you get!
Laura, late sixties, widow

■ ■ ■

There's something wrong with this online business if men tell me I shouldn't be posting photos of me and my daughter because dating sites are all about you and not family. I did delete them only because guys wanted to know who the cute redhead standing next to me in front of the Eiffel Tower was.
CP, fifties, divorced

■ ■ ■

One—don't date any man wearing shades! He's hiding something. Two— check photos carefully for pieces of arms on shoulders because you can bet he's tried to crop out his wife or girlfriend.
Donna, sixty-eight, divorced

■　■　■

I tell everyone, a single picture is enough and it has to be recent, like in the last couple months. The last thing you want is your date walking into a room and saying you're not the person they e-mailed. Oh, and another reason why you should not overwhelm anyone with photos…your essence should look better than the picture.
Helen, fifties, divorced

■　■　■

In his photos (neck up) he looked like an attractive man; in person he was about 300 lbs. I'm not athletic, toned, or slender. I am a soft, voluptuous, curvy, zaftig woman who has a constant 20 lb challenge, so I am not looking for a Greek God. If I can be honest in my description, I can't understand why men can't provide an honest one of themselves and have photos to verify.
Nan, fifty-nine, divorced

■　■　■

I must address the reality of how important the visual is in attracting men. That's why I've paid particular attention to the two photos I've posted. The "sunglasses" one was taken this past May. The "cabin" photo was taken up in the Smokies, Autumn 2015. I send it only to confirm that I am, in fact, very petite. This works both ways in terms of attraction…for some it is great, and for others, not enough…so I leave that up to you…I hope for you, the former…
LCN, sixties, divorced

■　■　■

My daughter put me on; otherwise, I wouldn't have had the nerve. The only problem, she posted pictures of the both of us. I think she put up five or six, some going back to when she was in high school. There was one when she graduated college, another when she got married, and one when she invited me on her boat with his husband. I was wearing a wetsuit, goggles. If it wasn't for one of the men who was kind enough to respond to me when I asked why he had rejected me, I wouldn't have known there was a problem.
How do you mean, problem?
My daughter is gorgeous. Men stop and stare at her whenever we're together. I don't exist. Get it?
Karen P, late fifties, divorced

■　■　■

This is how photos can get you into trouble. I'm not getting any responses until one day I'm with my daughter at a Yankee game, and she says I look so good, why doesn't she take a picture of me, so I can post it on my profile? Two days later, I'm getting tons of responses. I figure it's my picture, right? Wrong? The first two outright lied when they said they were lawyers, but were really ticket brokers. The third was a ticket scalper. I had my daughter take photos in the park; posted them, met a guy who happens to be a Red Sox's fan. Can't have everything, I guess.
Laura N, late sixties, divorced

■　■　■

What to Expect Now

■ ■ ■

We think we can play with love,
but we are mistaken.
Love plays with us.

—C. P. (ONLINE VETERAN)

YOU'VE FOLLOWED MY advice and ensured you posted the best possible photo(s) and he liked them! To continue, you must understand there are three types of guys you will encounter and anticipate how each of them will react to your overtures.

The first type, let's call him *Shallow Hal,* is so besotted by your images, he will immediately contact you. Looks are everything to *Shallow Hal,* so he doesn't need to read the rest of your profile, and therefore, he doesn't care one wit if he misses the news that you're presently locked in a cell in Albania and need a thousand dollars to gain your freedom. (Just saying…)

The second type, let's call him *Cautious Shallow Hal,* is no less enamored with your photos, but he's either been burnt before or just a little bit more careful. This gent will scan your profile, and if there's nothing in there about Albania (just saying)—he'll make contact.

(*Warning! All men seek perfection. I know what you're thinking. How can someone so imperfect be such a jerk? Get over it. That's the way it is, so let's make sure we don't show him any blemishes.*)

The third type is *Substance Man.* He finds you just as attractive as the other two, but understands your looks are just the beginning, and there is much more to sustaining a meaningful relationship. *This is the keeper!*

Unfortunately, like the rest of his species, he's searching for perfection and will search your profile hunting for those ugly red flags until he's convinced you are *The One*. Stick with me, and let's make sure that happens.

Men, this wouldn't be a fair and objective guide unless I describe the types of women you will face on the Internet. So I diligently went about examining my own experiences and then talked to numerous fellow travelers in an exhausting effort to gather their insights.

Something amazing happened. I don't know if our metaphoric hard drives were erased, or the simple fact was—there just isn't a *Shallow* or *Cautious Sally* among their species—just one *Substance Lady* after another...!

Guys, all I can say is continue to be the gentlemen our moms taught us to be when she first sent us out into the world, and remember...mothers always know best.

■　■　■

Figured it couldn't be any worst than walking into a bar where you didn't know anyone. Just took your chances and looked for a friendly face. I'm not crazy, wouldn't go into a biker bar, so I picked a site that looked like it had relatively normal women. Good-looking but not dangerous, if you get my drift?
Ellyn, late fifties, divorced

■　■　■

I really didn't know what to expect, but I wanted to be real. I mean, show guys who I really was. What they saw on the profile was what they were going to get. I knew how important pictures are in showing what you're capable of. I took some on the boardwalk, posing waist-high in a bathing suit, so they could see I liked having fun, and they could also see my figure. Also took some in sporty outfits, so they saw I was active. I made sure my essay reflected that part of my life. Give them the whole package. You know—truth in advertising.
C, sixty-nine, widow

■　■　■

I just put myself out there. I knew there were all sorts of men in cyberspace, but I said, what the heck! I wrote, I live life to the fullest with a joie de vivre! I said I enjoy travel and am ready for my next trip: Europe, Mexico, Florida, tropical islands, Vegas, ski resorts, Aspen, and many, many more! I added I love film, most kinds of music, concerts, theater, dancing, gambling, health spas, working out, sports (I love the Yankees and Mets). Tennis is a passion. Like I said, I let it all go and gave it the old college try.
FC, fifty-nine, divorced

■　■　■

Things have a separate reality on dating sites. What I mean is, you e-mail all the time. Messages flying back and forth, every couple of minutes. You start to expect this immediacy, and then it comes to meeting in real life, real time, and she's late. OK, you let it slide, but then it keeps happening, and you realize the online experience got its own separate reality based on how attached you are to your devices and how fast you get your fingers to move on the keyboard. That's a lot different than setting up an actual real time and place to meet and getting there when you're supposed, and this person just couldn't do that. I wanted to tell her she'd be late for her own funeral, but I was too much of a gentleman.
Hank, sixties, widower

■　■　■

The Essay

■ ■ ■

At the touch of love everyone becomes a poet.

—PLATO

WOMEN, THIS IS the section you'll excel in more than men because you can be forthright, honest, and vulnerable. You can wax poetically about the exotic locales that have broadened your world view. You will open your heart about the family you cherish and the lifelong friends you adore. You will fervently list the music, literature, art, and cuisines that nourish your soul. These are the things you love, that make life worth living, and you hope are as important to him, as they are to you.

(Warning! While Substance Man will read your essay, even he will succumb to his baser instincts and first check out your measurements.)

Guys—you're not twenty-one anymore, and you can't get away with immature stuff like getting kicks from racing your Harley up against a Mustang on the Long Island Expressway at four in the morning.

No bullshit, either. Not when they're all sorts of fact-checking sites that will turn up everything from your financials to whether or not you even have a passport. (Makes it harder to have that house in the South of Spain if you don't have one, right—knucklehead?)

Men—I guess what I'm saying is try to get in touch with that *sensitive side* and take a page out of the ladies' playbook.

(Strike that! Eric—Are you nuts? Didn't your publisher tell you if you used "man" and "sensitive" in the same sentence, you'd lose 90 percent of the male readership?)

■ ■ ■

Do: Understand the difference between *Call me Ishmael* and *Call Me Stud Muffin.*

■ ■ ■

Do: Be positive. He can sense negativity when you write, "I'd rather bang my head against the wall, than fill out this profile."

■ ■ ■

Do: Be honest. If breaking bricks with your bare hands is a deal breaker, he'd better find out here, rather than on YouTube.

■ ■ ■

Don't: Talk about your chats with Cleopatra. You're writing for a dating site, not the *Twilight Zone.*

■ ■ ■

Don't: Flout mechanical prowess. Anyone who can fieldstrip a weapon in the dark *is* intimidating.

■ ■ ■

Don't: Declare *I love walking on the beach at sunset.* That's code for *buy me a house in the Hamptons.*

■ ■ ■

Don't: Be a drama queen. I said, write a good opening sentence: "Give me a good man or give me death?" Really?

■ ■ ■

Begin with: *Everyone thinks I look like…*get it straight; only his opinion counts, not the one coming from your manicurist.

■ ■ ■

Don't: Be a *nurse.* Unless you're Florence Nightingale, you don't want him showing up attached to a portable oxygen tank.

■ ■ ■

Don't: Be a *purse.* Unless you want him to sponge off you, save the bit about oil being discovered in your backyard for your memoires.

■ ■ ■

Don't: Go against your nature. If he doesn't like sweet, sensitive, nurturing, nourishing…*f-him and the horse he rode in on.*

■ ■ ■

Don't: Begin with: *You should see me in a Speedo.* Guys—Speedo and being over sixty-five shouldn't be in the same profile, unless you're on steroids.

■   ■   ■

Don't: Use three-syllable words. Unless you want him to feel more insecure than he already is, why waste *five-dollar words on a two-cent dictionary?*

■   ■   ■

Don't: Beat around the bush. If you want a boy toy just say it, instead of bragging how you love to serve your man milk and cookies in bed.

■   ■   ■

Don't: Talk shop. Certainly she'll be impressed you work for the CDC, but do you think she's going to jump into bed with someone who just handled Anthrax?

■   ■   ■

Don't: Spout any words of wisdom. While it might be true *revenge is best served cold,* it can lead men to think your late husband didn't die of natural causes.

■   ■   ■

Don't: Come on like gangbusters. A*ttractive, adventuresome, accomplished, intelligent, and intellectual;* please save the breast-beating for the next sentence.

■   ■   ■

Don't: Be overly sentimental. She doesn't want to know you cried for a month when your favorite beer manufacturer turned wimpy and made a light beer.

■　■　■

Don't: Copy your college essay. So it got you into Harvard? Unless you can fit into your cheerleader's outfit and still do those splits, he won't give two rah-rahs.

■　■　■

Don't: Be wordy. The difference between liking jazz and saying it ignites a rhapsody of flame within the fiber of my being is the difference between reading the rest of your essay and becoming nauseous.

■　■　■

Absolutely Do Not: Use emojis. I know, I warned you before, but don't give into temptation and put one in after you mentioned your fondness for group sex. 😊

■　■　■

If he can't spell—end of story for me. No excuse, not with spell checker. Oh, and one-word answers, those guys are just as bad.
Helen, fifties, divorced

■　■　■

It may have been love at first sight for him, but he got me in his essay. It was funny. I'm a fool for funny, and he was funny.
Karen P, late fifties, divorced

■　■　■

33

I'm thinking about having someone professional write my essay. A friend had it done, and she got herself a boyfriend almost immediately.
Donna, sixty-eight, divorced

■ ■ ■

You do intrigue me, you know. It takes a particularly quirky mind to concoct such a bio. Mine's nowhere as innovative. But read it, if you will. And check out my non-Botoxed pictures.
NCB, fifty-nine, divorced

■ ■ ■

I almost stopped reading your profile, because it was "unusual," but I'm glad I finished it to the end. I got a good laugh out of it. Zut alors! (Couldn't resist the French.) Hey, I'm a downtown kind of gal, wouldn't know a Manolo unless he was the waiter in a Mexican restaurant. No dead husbands that I know about. But who's keeping score? Have you seen any good movies lately?
Karen P, late fifties, divorced

■ ■ ■

Actually, my not-yet-friend, but definitely kindred soul, your profile was a delight to read. Thank you for making me smile, for being smart, funny, and creative company. In an "encounter" such as this, I feel I can have "great" fun just being myself, knowing whatever strange machinations my brain comes up with, will be taken the "right" way! You have, in a very positive sense, removed the shackles and loosed the fateful whirlwind. (How's that for a mix?) Take cover! Or, alternatively, write me back.
GGG, sixty-five, widow

■ ■ ■

Hi—great profile—made me smile. Can't guarantee the bells and whistles (chemistry thing), but it will be a fun meeting. Let me put you at ease, tell you no I'm not a barmaid by trade, as photo might suggest, and adorable kids and dog are not rentals to make me look good. Seriously, hope you'd like to say a formal "hi" to me.
KK, late fifties, widow

■　■　■

To know me is to like me. I am multi-talented. A retired CPA who has returned to my earlier passion, oils. Been married, widowed, and recently lost a remarkable woman I connected with on this site and hopeful the magic repeats. I find that as I grow older, I continue to love learning and exploring new ideas with people as devoted to personal growth as I. Empathetic and seek the essence of intimacy with a woman who can handle that kind of man.
Gavin, seventy-two, widower

■　■　■

The Yes/No and Check Here Sections

■ ■ ■

Love looks not with the eyes,
but with the mind, and therefore
is wing'd cupid painted blind.

—WILLIAM SHAKESPEARE, *A MIDSUMMER NIGHT'S DREAM*

BECAUSE THE PEOPLE running dating sites are fostering the notion we all have the retention span of a moth, the questions in these sections resemble those given to second graders.

Innocent as they appear, they carried hidden meanings and are potential red flags. For example, in the Body Type category, full-figured or well-rounded translates into having no idea what *portion control* means.

As previously noted, each website is different, but the following headers seem typical to all: General Info, Physical Attributes, My Background, My LifeStyle, and My Ideal Match.

Ladies—don't think these sections are a place to vent. Remarks like "Unless you're married, the touch of his hand makes you jump" and "I avoid eye contact, because men will rape you with their eyes," are uncalled for.

Guys—stuff like "Nobody in my family covers their mouth when they sneeze" and "The sooner the kid's an earner, the sooner it's worth having 'em" are also no-nos.

(Warning! Lies always catch up with you, and the last thing you want is to answer a nonsmoker here, and in another section, rave nothing goes better with a brandy than a Cohiba.)

■ ■ ■

Need to talk to him on the phone, see if he can put a sentence together.
CP, fifties, divorced

■ ■ ■

I don't flirt. I don't like the "Secret Admirer Category." I don't like the short answer sections. I did get a big kick out of your..."In my own words and the 'About me section.'"
Nan, fifty-nine, divorced

■ ■ ■

No longer amazed, upset, humiliated, disappointed by the Q&A. I guess it's par for the course guys ask you to show up in three-inch stilettos, showing cleavage.
Gloria, fifty-five, widow

■ ■ ■

Not one for details, so I liked yes/no sections. Figured most men lied anyway. At least that's why real-life has taught me, and so far things online don't seem to be any different.
Helen, fifties, divorced

■ ■ ■

I don't like to spend a lot of time on these questions, and I wish the whole thing was like this. I don't know any guy who wants to waste his time writing a lot of bullshit. We just want to find a pretty woman.
Jack, fifty-nine, widower

■   ■   ■

You know the old saying: A picture is worth a thousand words? That's all I need. Maybe a couple of yes and no's just to see if they live close by. I'm too old to drive more than twenty miles for any woman.
C, sixty-nine, widow

■   ■   ■

I picked eHarmony because I'm interested in finding out if we are compatible, and it's only through a series of detailed questions, I believe I can find my soul mate. So far this has worked for me. The men I have dated are interesting, and although I haven't found Mr. Right, I believe this is the right approach for me.
Ellyn, late fifties, divorced

■   ■   ■

At my age, I don't have a lot of patience, so my answer to you is yes. I wish all these sites just had yes and no questions. I don't want to spend a lot of time thinking about what I need to say to impress a woman. Same goes for what she writes. It's not that I'm not interested. It's like I told you in the beginning, I don't have a lot of patience. Maybe it's a concentration thing...
FC, fifty-nine, divorced

■   ■   ■

I felt it was important to tell the women, although I've have had some great relationships that, for a bunch of reasons never resulted in marriage and children, didn't mean I wasn't interested in marriage or being part of her extended

family. I didn't want women to think I couldn't commit or that I didn't like kids...in our cases, grown ones...
AC, sixty-nine, widower

■　■　■

I was a literature major back when I went to college. Always fancied myself as a writer, even though, I became a pharmacist. I really like the essay, and as far as these yes and no questions, I like to add little quips wherever I can. I'm happy to say the women find my essay and these little extras appealing and provocative. I shouldn't be telling you all this. Giving away all my secrets. Guys will start to follow my example and give me competition.
Ben, sixty plus, divorced

■　■　■

General Information

∎ ∎ ∎

You know you're in love when you can't fall asleep,
because reality is finally better than your dreams.

—DR. SEUSS

REMEMBER WHAT I just wrote about innocent-looking questions and their hidden meanings? I was speaking in overall terms. This is the first section you will actually be put to the test, so give it your full attention and don't answer carelessly, as this will result in the dreaded red flag and the viewer's early exit.

Again, let me remind you not to be put off by how inane some of these questions appear. Remember, too, what it says in the Bible—forgive them for they know not what they do.

(Warning! That doesn't mean you'll be forgiven if you don't follow my Dos and Don'ts. To quote another line from the Bible: Hell hath no fury than an author's scorn.)

∎ ∎ ∎

I was so terrified my pictures weren't good that I really didn't pay attention to the rest of the site and just put down the first thing that came into my head.
Donna, sixty-eight, divorced

∎ ∎ ∎

I recounted my experiences of dealing with someone sideswiping my car and how I got their insurance to pay for it. This was great stuff because I got women contacting me to help them get the same results.
Jack, fifties, divorced

■ ■ ■

Everybody lies, so I did. I shouldn't say lie. I mean, fib a little like telling my real age. All the girls told me to take off five years, never ever say sixty when you can say fifty-nine. That's not so bad. Besides, guys do it too. They're even worst. No hair, no money, and overweight. Don't get me started.
KK, late fifties, widow

■ ■ ■

I heard some women change their identity for each site. That's crazy. I'm a player, and I want women to know it. I lay it on really thick. Make sure they understand where I'm coming from. Oh, I listen to what they say. Like, no more pictures of me without a shirt. Another thing; stay clear of a woman who shows off her cleavage because they just paid for it, and they're looking for a sugar daddy to make them whole again.
Steve, late sixties, divorced

■ ■ ■

Online Now

■ ■ ■

Don't forget I'm just a girl,
standing in front of a boy,
asking him to love her.

—ANNA, *NOTTING HILL*

SEE—SEE—DIDN'T I tell you? Right away these wizards of romance are playing with your head. Online now? Of course you're online, or else you couldn't be filling out the questionnaire!

(Warning! Remember who you are and don't be goateed into giving them a snarky reply!)

Regardless of your gender, like Anna from *Notting Hill,* do not forget you have the courage and the sense of humor to put yourself out there in search of love and romance! No red flags, here...ladies and gentlemen!

■ ■ ■

Do: Say yes. Demonstrates you know how to multitask.

■ ■ ■

Don't: Be maudlin and cry *where else can I find love if not here?*

■ ■ ■

Don't: Be desperate and declare *so many men, so little time.*

■ ■ ■

Don't: Curry favor and proclaim *this is the place for love.*

■ ■ ■

Don't: Be sappy and lament, "I go where my virtual heart takes me."

■ ■ ■

Don't: Capitalize *yes* and repeat it five times. I know you don't have a life, but he doesn't have to know it.

■ ■ ■

Don't: Think you're tweeting and decide to use all one hundred forty characters when a simple *yes* or *no* will do.

■ ■ ■

Don't: Express your true feelings, especially here by declaring that you'd have a better chance of getting hit by lightning than finding a halfway decent guy online.

■ ■ ■

Absolutely Do Not: Say I am not an addict and I can go offline anytime I choose.

■ ■ ■

I like the cut of your jibe. If you like to cruise and sounds like you do online now.
Mel, fifties, divorced (twice)

■　■　■

Hate the little alert that tells you they're "Online Now" or "Ready to Chat." Too intimidating.
Laura, late sixties, widow

■　■　■

Crossed-eyed, but no cross-dresser...OK, so I'm not crossed-eyed...You sound just as nutty as I. Would love to compare medications. Am online now.
CW, sixties, widow

■　■　■

You don't know me that well, but I can tell you although I appear to be "proper," I am not at all. Please don't delete until you respond back. Online now!
Ellyn, late fifties, divorced

■　■　■

I'm a grown woman. Was in business. I've raised a family. Had a successful marriage. Been through a lot, but I have to confess, nothing terrified me more than this. Maybe it's my generation.
Donna, sixty-eight, divorced

■　■　■

Fellow cat lover, I sleep with three cats. As you, I love opera, Daniel Silva and NPR. High points on your "in common scale," don't you agree? Check me out further and see what you think. PS online now so, do it, if you're going to do it.
Gloria, fifty-five, widow

■   ■   ■

All the bars in my neighborhood closed up. What choice did I have? Had to go online. I'm into computer programming, so the process was a snap. I may go a little overboard and stay online too long, but I always stayed till the bars closed so this is nothing new.
Steve, sixties, divorced

■   ■   ■

Your Age

■ ■ ■

Love has no age,
no limit;
and no death.

—JOHN GALSWORTHY

I DIDN'T LIE...EVERYONE says I look younger than my age. If they hadn't, and if I didn't want to believe them, I would have shaved off five, maybe ten years. I can't believe I just confessed this. In fact, it's the first time I've realized what my motivation was. It's true. *There's no fool like an old fool.*

Men—remember, women aren't like trees, so no added remarks like: *You can tell a woman's age by her wrinkles.* No left-handed compliments either like: *I'm impressed your breasts defy the laws of gravity, natural selection, and age.*

Women—you've all told me you take five years off on principle. One or two have confessed it was one of the guilty pleasures they received for being online; that after a while, they actually felt the lie made them feel younger.

Finally, I'm reminded of the Mark Twain saying one of my interviewees threw at me when I broached this topic. *Age is an issue of mind over matter. If you don't mind, it doesn't matter.*

■ ■ ■

Do: Be true to thyself. Unlike men, you won't feel good about yourself until you confess, so save yourself the anxiety, and don't shave off more than *five years.*

■ ■ ■

Don't: Approximate. Sixty-five is *not* almost sixty.

■ ■ ■

Don't: Declare *beauty is in the eyes of the beholder—so behold!*

■ ■ ■

Don't: Listen to friends. There's a reason the girls at Mahjong are all single.

■ ■ ■

Don't: Check your birth certificate; it'll give you less confidence when you lie.

■ ■ ■

Don't: Trust your hairdresser. Thirty-five? And you wonder why you overtip?

■ ■ ■

Don't: Write *young at heart.* It will only remind him he needs to get his annual.

■ ■ ■

Don't: Pretend to be fifty and then say you cried the day Bobby Thomson hit the homer that beat the Dodgers back in 1951.

■　■　■

Don't: Write *age doesn't matter*. In other words, you want someone with one foot in the grave.

■　■　■

Don't: Don't be a wiseass. Fifty-something! Come on, you cannot make *something out of nothing!*

■　■　■

Don't: Be coy. He wants to *see* your answer, not *hear* it in the sound of your voice.

■　■　■

Don't: Employ *The New Math*. You may hear *seventy is the new sixty* but that doesn't add up.

■　■　■

Don't: Forget, if you posted a pic of you winning the over seventies' tennis trophy, you can't write down fifty-nine.

■　■　■

Don't: Be a comedian. Jack Benny got his audience to laugh by staying thirty-nine forever, but you're not that funny.

■　■　■

Don't: Underestimate his intelligence. He might not know the names of the seasons, but he knows you're not younger than springtime.

■ ■ ■

Don't: Be a *niner*. You're sixty-one, but he wants fifty-sixty, so you write fifty-nine. *Fool me once, shame on you. Fool me twice, shame on me.*

■ ■ ■

Don't: Add...and don't I look good for my age? Never ask a question you don't know the answer to. (Anyone who's seen *Law & Order* knows that.)

■ ■ ■

Don't: Rely on self-help books. OK, they preach *you're as young as you feel* but *sixty going on sixteen?*

■ ■ ■

Don't: Be poetic and declare: *Like a succulent piece of fruit, I had to ripen before picked.* Picked you will be—by men you'll eventually pick out of a police lineup.

■ ■ ■

Absolutely Do Not: Tamper with your driver's license. Just go to Staples. There's nothing those kids can't do when it comes to Photoshop.

■ ■ ■

I am also slightly above the age parameters that you indicated, so if you are open to a still-younger-than-you awesome lady…
Donna, sixty-eight, divorced

■　■　■

Growing old is inevitable, getting old is an option, and when I find a man who has that mantra, I'm going to chase him down.
Helen, fifties, divorced

■　■　■

I'm fun to be with. Very spirited for my age and fairly attractive. I love adventure, good conversation; a loving, romantic partner with radical honesty. Are you out there? Write to me.
NCB, fifty-nine, divorced

■　■　■

I'm seventy-four and keep getting e-mails from men half my age who say they want a "hook-up." When I asked a sixty-year-old married friend what that meant, he told me. When I became angry, he calmed me down, told me how attractive I was and how I should think it over. I did, and it's not happening.
HG, seventy-four, widow

■　■　■

After a few flirts that I didn't respond to, she wrote: "You need a facelift." When I tried to check her out, I discovered she was no longer on the site. She could have had the courage of her convictions and stayed long enough to see my reply. What would I have said? I agree…
The Author

■　■　■

If I get another "Young at Heart" I am going to quit this online dating thing forever. Don't men and I guess women, too, although I don't see their profiles, realize how being original is so important? Has age dulled our brains to the point we can't come up with something more provocative, more appealing?

Laura, late sixties, widow

· · ·

On the one hand, I am too old for you...DOB 5/1/40. On the other hand, if your details are accurate, we have a lot in common...however...I am terrible at racquet sports. My personality is pretty much as you described yours. It would be great to take a walk in the park and find out if we are truth tellers.

BL, seventy-four, widower

· · ·

It's a given I'm going to lie. Shave off a few years. I don't see the harm. Men do it, too, believe me. Maybe more than women. I do agree we have to confess the truth, but I like to play it by ear. If I see things are getting serious, I slip it in. If not, why ruin the illusion, especially if the gentleman continues to flatter me, remind me of how young I look.

Ellyn, late fifties, divorced

· · ·

This one sharp cutie caught me by complete surprise when he asked me questions about when I graduated high school. I don't know what made him suspect I lied about my age? Maybe, he's the suspicious kind? Maybe he had ESP? Got all flustered, gave him the real dates. What a screw-up! The moral is to be like a Girl Scout and always be prepared!

Linda, sixties, widow

· · ·

I write sixty-five to seventy-five and guys in the eighties show up. In the beginning I took them to task. Now, I just don't say anything, accept one drink or cup of coffee, then excuse myself and leave. I'm not saying some aren't interesting. I met several who would have given me the moon, but I'm not in it for the next three months. Also, most couldn't walk around the block without a walker, and at sixty I'm not ready to go that route.
Laura, late sixties, widow

■ ■ ■

I'm fifty-nine, and that's the truth. I run deep. Life can be fun, but some things have to be taken seriously. Commitment to friends and family means a lot to me. I enjoy doing fun things, but am always there to help with life's curve balls. Oh, and as you can see by my photos, I look younger than my age, and that's the face I was born with. No surgery, Botox, etc, etc...
Nan, fifty-nine, divorced

■ ■ ■

I'm seven-three, look good for my age and don't have problem meeting men. Normally, we have dinner, and if we hit it off, begin the journey. Never had any act rude or impolite way, except one. Right away, he says, I know you want to have sex. When I asked what made him think that, he said all widowed women my age, probably had sex with only one man, now wanted to experience sex again; and he was there to satisfy them. He winked, bragged he was ten for ten. I winked back, told him I wasn't going to be number eleven.
A, seventy-three, widow

■ ■ ■

Physical Attributes

■ ■ ■

I want you. All of you. Your flaws.
Your mistakes. Your imperfections.
I want you, and only you.

—(Unknown)

REMEMBER WHAT I said about *Shallow Guys* and how even *Substance Man* would jump from your photos to your bust size? Why some of them may even print out your measurements to make sure they jibe with the rest of your profile. Let 'em! Let 'em make copies! Follow my advice, and all they will find is perfection and their printer alerting them to the disturbing fact, *they've run out of ink!*

And forget about whether you think you're desirable or not. What's the saying, *there's a top for every pot*? My friend Mike likes *a lot of meat on his tomatoes* (talk about mixing metaphors). He loves to disappear into his *Big Mamma's arms*. Other men friends want their women *paper thin*.

I've met some so frail I'm afraid if they grabbed hold of a balloon string, a stiff wind would lift them up and blow them into the next county.

Women—I know you're always talking relationships, but I've interviewed several vets who used *buff* and *six-pack abs* more than once when saying the man didn't necessarily need to have them at our age, but it would be nice.

■ ■ ■

I kid you not. The first thing out of her mouth when we met in person, "Tell me the truth, you couldn't tell from my picture, could you?" When I looked confused, she continued. "Face lifts…come on, tell me, how many facelifts do you think I've had." Not enough, but I was too much of a gentleman to say it.
Jack, fifty-nine, widower

■ ■ ■

He had a hook! Don't you think that's the kind of thing you'd mention in your essay? What about on the phone or in e-mails? Nothing even remotely close to him revealing a disability…we planned on a drink, then he wanted to add dinner, finally a jazz show. Normally, I don't want to put myself into a situation where I have to spend a lot of time with someone I've never met, but we got along so nicely, figured I'd take a chance. Imagine seeing someone walk in with a hook for a right hand? He took it off during dinner, hid it with a black handkerchief when he entered the jazz club. A real crapshoot, this Internet business, huh?
Linda, sixties, widow

■ ■ ■

Your Height

■ ■ ■

We all know that when the lights are out,
all women are the same height

—Patrick Rothfuss, *The Wise Man's Fear*

The women I've talked with don't have a problem with height, except maybe wanting to be a little taller, and that's easily fixable, although a lifetime of wearing heels has sent many to the chiropodist, leaving them with no choice.

I have a different tale of the tape to tell. The day before I signed up, I had my yearly physical. Now—I'm five eight. That's the number on my driver's license, passport, and on my lips whenever anyone asks. All my adult life I've been five eight. I wouldn't be Eric if I weren't five eight.

"Five seven," she chirped as she viewed the mark on the scale.

Bullshit! Bullshit! Bullshit! I didn't lose an inch since the last time I was here!

No, I didn't say that! *And no,* I didn't show her my driver's license or ask her to measure me again. She was going to be taking my blood, and you don't piss off anyone who's going to stick a needle into your vein.

I was still cursing to myself when it came to filling out the profile. Then I remember the words of my mother when she sent me off to school on that very first day. *Stand up straight, Ricky. Stand up straight if you want people to see how tall you are.* Damn right—I wrote five eight!

■ ■ ■

Do: Remember—you do not count the height of your hair.

■　■　■

Do: Write out feet and inches. Apostrophes will only confuse him.

■　■　■

Do: Know the difference between getting him excited and telling the truth. *Thunder thighs* do not make a woman taller.

■　■　■

Don't: Answer in *centimeters* and show him you're *un-American.*

■　■　■

Don't: Be intimidating. Stuff like a *dancer's legs* will scare off the wallflowers.

■　■　■

Don't: Beg the issue by saying *you have great calves.* Come on, at four feet, the only way they'd look great is if you walked on stilts.

■　■　■

Don't: Use Tom Cruise unless you're as handsome or intend to stand on an apple crate when you're with her.

■　■　■

Don't: Measure yourself in stilettos or lifts. Unless you plan on never taking them off, I'd take off the extra four inches.

■ ■ ■

Don't: Say you have legs that never quit. He probably doesn't know the expression and will confuse you with the Energizer Bunny.

■ ■ ■

Don't: Use Napoleon as a sex symbol. First of all, you're not the emperor of France, and second of all...oh hell, there's no second of all!

■ ■ ■

Don't: Point out you're so small, he could put you in his overnight bag. This is code for *take me to Paris tonight!* (Or, you have an eating disorder.)

■ ■ ■

Don't: Cite the *Kama Sutra* if you're under five feet. Sure women look tiny in those diagrams, but don't put yourself in a *position* you'll only regret, later.

■ ■ ■

Don't: Say you played high-school basketball when we all know, back in the day, no player reached the rim unless they were standing on a teammate's shoulder.

■ ■ ■

Absolutely Do Not: Proclaim *taller women don't intimidate real men*. If you want to question his manhood, why don't you just ask him if he eats quiche?

■　■　■

I'm losing inches by the year. Fortunately, the women are as well.
Gavin, seventy-two, widower

■　■　■

If you can handle a woman in four-inch Manolos, my number is (---)(---)(----).
GGG, sixty-five, widow

■　■　■

You do intrigue me, you know. It takes a particularly quirky mind to concoct such a bio. Mine's nowhere as innovative. Am two inches taller. Will that be a problem?
Karen P, late fifties, divorced

■　■　■

Sixty-five and still active, play basketball twice a week at the Y, and from your picture and profile looks like you're tall enough and in good shape, too. Let's get together for some round ball.
Larry, sixty-five, widower

■　■　■

Just over five feet, but I still believe in the magic that can happen when you meet someone with whom you connect. If you don't mind tiny women, know how to love and to laugh, we just might make magic together.
Gloria, fifty-five, widow

■　■　■

The thing I hate most about dating women my age is they've all shrunk. And they don't want to wear high heels to make them look taller. All I hear is they've worn heels all their lives and now it just about comfort. I think they should make allowances for when they go out on date. I do. I wear cowboy boots and they make me look a couple of inches taller.
Jack, fifty-nine, widower

■   ■   ■

I've always been tall, so when I started dating, I picked guys who I could look up to. Good bone structure runs in my family, so aging hasn't affected my height, whereas, it's done the opposite to men my age. I'm seriously thinking of going ten years younger. A girl gets tired of staring down at a guy's baldhead.
Helen, fifties, divorced

■   ■   ■

I'm just over five feet, and I like men about my height. I always make that clear and reassure any guy I speak that being short is OK. I'll call him Gene. Lived nearby, nice photo, although when I checked it after we met, I realized it wasn't full-figured. I think you see where this is going. Anyway, we agree to meet at a hotel bar in our neighborhood. I'm waiting, look up, see a guy waving, can't believe my eyes—he's a dwarf! When he sees my surprise, he stands up, shows me he's five-feet. Only problem, a third of his body is his head. We have a drink, nice conversation and figure, if he calls me again, I won't turn him down just because he's—you know…he never calls…
GGG, sixty-five, widow

■   ■   ■

Your Weight

■ ■ ■

Dear God—if you can't make me thin,
make my friends fat!

—Anonymous

As promised, the dreaded *weight question.* I've given you plenty of *Dos* and *Don'ts,* so I'm confident you can handle it with a smile on your face; but if you want to take a moment, a day, even a week—be my guest. This is your profile!

It's my theory, unproven of course, but I believe women know their weight to the very ounce. Every woman I've met seems to bear this out. So does the testimony of the many men I've talked to during the course of reaching this book.

On the other hand, women have told me the opposite. Could it be men are so ignorant, or do we just lie with such impunity?

Women point to how overweight men always hide their bellies by posting pictures of their faces or placing themselves behind a barbeque grill, walnut desk, or the wheel of a sports car.

Several of the men I interviewed seemed guilty of doing just this, but when I asked them why they had chosen those particular poses, they looked at me like I was talking to them in a foreign language.

I have come to the realization that the men to whom I spoke with, were indeed, completely oblivious to their own proportions; however, they were keenly aware of a woman's waistline, even calling themselves *Chubby Chasers, Skinny Seekers, or Polecats.*

I know…I know…but nobody said life is fair or promised you a rose garden.

■   ■   ■

Do: Realize they are asking for your *real*, not your *ideal* weight.

■   ■   ■

Do: Be truthful. Has anyone ever referred to your looks as *wispy*?

■   ■   ■

Don't: Write *whippet-like* unless you want him to bring a leash.

■   ■   ■

Don't: Use kilograms. I forgot, she'll also think you're a drug smuggler.

■   ■   ■

Don't: Boast. You'd look like Brad Pitt if he gained two hundred pounds.

■   ■   ■

Don't: Admit the only place to get an accurate reading is at a weigh station.

■   ■   ■

Don't: Use kilograms. Just like the use of *centimeters*, very *un-American*.

■   ■   ■

Don't: Capitalize. *Attention Chubby Chasers* will draw enough attention without putting it in all-caps.

■　■　■

Don't: Think you can call yourself *Tiny Tina* when you're wearing a dress made by *Omar the Tentmaker.*

■　■　■

Don't: Declare *I'm so slim you won't even know I'm there.* Tell me, how can he show you off, if you're invisible?

■　■　■

Don't: Boast how much you'll save him in food bills. Come on, we've all seen skinny women shovel in food twice their weight.

■　■　■

Don't: Think he's that stupid. Come on—there's more to love? Why don't you just write *elephant-like*—that's what's he's going to think anyway!

■　■　■

Don't: Brag how it only took a month after giving birth to return to your original weight, unless you can lose the extra three inches by next weekend.

■　■　■

Don't: Reference *Henry VIII? Stud-muffin, sure;* but he was the king for God sakes; and what about all the women he executed? Think man...think!

■　■　■

Absolutely Do Not: Show *before* and *after* photos. I don't care how sexy you look now, but it's the *before* pic that will make them lose their lunch.

■ ■ ■

There was a time I considered killing any woman who was thinner than I.
Donna, sixty-eight, divorced

■ ■ ■

Dear fellow jogger. Ready to join me for a 5k? Pasta afterward! Don't hesitate. Contact me.
Helen, fifties, divorced

■ ■ ■

I'm not thinking of joining a site for people of my size; however, I've always attracted Chubby Chasers, so I'm not sure what I'm going to do.
Gladys, sixty, divorced

■ ■ ■

My body looks pretty good in clothes, and when the lights are low; well—once you've seen stretch marks in the moonlight, you'll never go back.
CW, fifties, widow

■ ■ ■

I'm a big man and proud of it. Problem is, I've got some health issues, so that's the reason I left it blank and posted only one headshot.
Jack, fifty-nine, widower

■ ■ ■

I'm sixty-eight, Caucasian and a tad overweight. Have resources allowing me to travel and seek companion equally adventuresome. I'm making my mind up between "The Dark Princess" who has just turned thirty and has a body that makes me think Playboy Centerfold, and a former Miss Hawaii finalist, a little younger but wants to teach me to skydive.
Larry, sixties, divorced (twice)

■　■　■

We met for coffee. I swear, not the same guy. Came right out and said you don't look like your photo. He said it's an old picture. The more I looked, saw how bloated his face had become, knew it had to be medication or just wasn't him. Didn't say anything because he was nice, but couldn't get it out of my head if he'd switched another guy's pic for his. Blocked him because he kept e-mailing me.
FC, fifty-nine, divorced

■　■　■

I'm a personal trainer and a diet coach. All the info is in my profile. I get an e-mail from this guy, let's call him, Bill. Nice-looking. No full-figure photos, but he says he's tall and slim, exercises regularly, and eats healthy. Seemed like a potential match. I talked to him on the phone. No red flags. We agreed to meet for coffee. The guy shows up, must be fifty/seventy pounds overweight. I'm amazed. I asked why he lied? He says he wanted me to help him lose weight. I asked how he thought any relationship could start off with a lie. He couldn't answer me. I got up and I left.
Helen, fifties, divorced

■　■　■

Your Body Type

■ ■ ■

Real beauty isn't about symmetry or weight or makeup;
It's about looking life right in the face
and seeing all its magnificence
reflected in your own.

—Valerie Monroe

Guys—I'm not sure you have to worry about this question because, speaking for myself, when I hear *body type*...I think cars.

Ladies—just because *me* and *mine* may give this question short shrift, doesn't imply you do as well. In fact, the opposite is true. You must guard against the possibility that *Shallow Hal* has printed out your photo and will compare it to your answers. You must double down. You can never be too wise, too clever, or use as many little white lies you think necessary.

(Warning! If you're watching your weight, don't go overboard and claim you use a thimble, not a scale, to weigh your food.)

■ ■ ■

Do: Look in the mirror to see if reality bites before you make your choice.

■ ■ ■

Don't: Say *Whippet-like.* Remember that warning about the leash?

■   ■   ■

Don't: Use terms like *rawboned;* obviously you have an eating disorder.

■   ■   ■

Don't: Confuse terms. I know you want to drop this one as often as you can, *but well endowed, however desirable, is not a body type!*

■   ■   ■

Don't: Use terms like *average* or *medium.* That's as bad as being called *nice,* and you know where *nice girls* finish?

■   ■   ■

Don't: Brag. If you can bounce a quarter off your abs, why aren't you dating someone from your gym?

■   ■   ■

Don't: Use terms *full-figured or well-rounded.* In other words, you have no idea what *portion control* means.

■   ■   ■

Don't: Use the term *wispy. Wispy, willowy;* he'll just think you blow away when he takes you outdoors.

■   ■   ■

Don't: Use analogies. *Man of Steel* (also a poor choice for a screen name), unless you can bend it like Superman.

■ ■ ■

Don't: Give him the wrong impression. You might be flexible, but don't say *it's the kind of body that keeps on giving;* he'll never let you leave the bedroom.

■ ■ ■

Don't': Use metaphors like *tough as nails* unless you're shaped like a stud.

■ ■ ■

Don't: Say *slim as a celery stick.* Here we go again with analogies that may confuse a meat eater.

■ ■ ■

Don't: Embellish. *Athletic/Fit* is enough, but do you always have to bring up those Olympic medals?

■ ■ ■

Absolutely Do Not: Come between him and his best friend. You've never met a *poll you couldn't slither down* but…the one in front of his house…and without asking if he has a dog…

■ ■ ■

Athletic. I'm seventy-eight and still play softball in a league for seniors, so why not?
Burt, seventy-eight, widower

■　■　■

Standard answers were very unflattering, so I wrote svelte. Thought that sounded better, less pretentious than elegantly slim.
Helen, fifties, divorced

■　■　■

Take a look. Nobody ever answers this question. And for good reason. The choices are too broad and certainly unflattering. Plus there's a very good chance you'll put yourself into a category that turns him off. Better to leave it blank. Will tell you later is too scary. So I would never choose that box.
Ellyn, late fifties, divorced

■　■　■

There is a reason I hate these sites and this question is one. I'm a guy, and I have no f-ing idea of what I'm supposed to write. Broad shoulders and thin waist? At sixty? Give me a break! I left it blank. So did all my friends except one who wrote, athletic, Like sitting in front of a TV watching the Mets makes this fat SOB athletic!
Hank, sixty, widower

■　■　■

Whatever cyberspace had in store for me, I just couldn't leave to fate. I had to take control, put more effort into losing weight. If I was going to use online dating to find a life partner, I had to make it like a work project. So, I made a business plan. Goals, strategy, implementation…things like that. It was more complicated but you get the idea. I discovered that once I put it together,

reviewed it, I had a good idea whether I could achieve my desired results. Even if you have no business experience, I suggest you go online, find the outline of a business plan and just change it around so your goal is to lose weight. You could even do it to find love on the Internet.
Chris, sixty-seven, divorced

■　■　■

It was the last week of my subscription, so I decided to go against my nature and go all wild and wicked. My girlfriends, all of who are in their late sixties as I am, called it nasty-girl. I changed my body type to curvaceous. I also took down my photos and replaced them with several very suggestive ones taken from profile so my breasts, that I recently had done, would be accentuated to its fullest. Something my old photos did not do. I also put on very skintight Lycra workout pants. I didn't change my hairstyle, essay, or anything else in my profile. I immediately received a ton of e-mails. So much so I renewed my subscription for another three months. Had many dates, several with men much younger than myself. No, I'm not going to say anymore.
Gloria, fifty-five, widow

■　■　■

I'm not into chubby, but he had a nice face so I said, why not? Believe it or not, first e-mail, one phone call, one date, love at first sight! Got married two months later. How's that for an endorsement!
Donna, late fifties, divorced

Your Hair Color

■ ■ ■

I never gave a lock of hair away,
To a man, Dearest, except this to thee...

—ELIZABETH BARRETT BROWNING

LIKE SO MANY of the men reading this book, I am a child of the two-dollar haircut. I still carry a *laissez faire attitude* toward hair grooming, although I confess, when I was in the ad game, I had to change my tune and spent serious money to keep stylishly ahead of the young bucks gunning for my job.

At that time, men were a rarity compared to women at these grooming palaces, and sitting in their presence made me realize what it took for them to be *au courant* in an ever-changing world of styles, colors, lengths, and other permutations that made my own hair stand on edge.

Please understand, I thoroughly appreciate your situation, and I want you to think of me as you would your hairdresser—and trust me when I say—he's going to love how your answers look.

I would be remiss if I didn't point out that my fellow male boomers are no longer strangers in a strange land when it comes to grooming and in particular, hair coloring. Just walk into any salon and observe the bodies wrapped in space-aged paraphernalia and tell me who's who.

I'm not only talking to the *silver foxes* but to the growing numbers of bleached blonde boomers trolling the boardwalks from Coney to Venice Beach.

So—men, let me say to you—she's going to love how your answers look.

■ ■ ■

Do: Look up the word *natural* before you use it, because there will come a time you'll show him your baby pictures.

■   ■   ■

Don't: Call it...*like a rainbow*. Unless he's into circus performers, he's long gone.

■   ■   ■

Don't: Forget he's a man. *Mousey Brown* will only make him call pest control.

■   ■   ■

Don't: Forget you're a man. *Mousey Brown...?*

■   ■   ■

Don't: Think *bald as a cue ball* is a hair color.

■   ■   ■

Don't: Go off message. Wild as the wind is not a color, either.

■   ■   ■

Don't: Confess *only my stylist knows*. He's not looking for references.

■   ■   ■

Don't: Think you're ordering coffee. Why else would describe it as *café noir?*

■   ■   ■

Don't: Write *dirty blonde*. Don't want him to know you're a *dirty girl*—not yet, anyway.

■   ■   ■

Don't: Confuse him by thinking *paint chips*. You're not at *Sherwin-Williams*, *so* why call it a vibrant hue of chocolate brown?

■   ■   ■

Don't: Name-drop. So…you and Bruce Willis had the same hair in *Die Hard* and now both are bald in *Good Day to Die Hard*. Yippee ki-yay, motherf***r!

■   ■   ■

Don't: Be risqué. *So soft to the touch, you'll want to stroke it all night long*, runs the risk of giving him a stroke before he has a chance to call you.

■   ■   ■

Absolutely Do Not: Wear a hat in your photos if you want to reference your full head of wavy hair. Duh.

■   ■   ■

One guy wrote mixed? What's up with that?
GGG, sixty-five, widow

■   ■   ■

I didn't mention I dye my hair. So far, no negatives, only compliments.
Hank, sixty, widower

■ ■ ■

I think women of a certain age shouldn't put streaks of purple into their hair,
but two girls at bridge swear it's the reason their e-mails increased.
Laura, late sixties, widow

■ ■ ■

Your Eye Color

■ ■ ■

Dark eyes make me melt, light eyes pull me in.
Brown eyes are my weakness,
blue eyes are my sin.

—WistfulHope

Tell me, what color are my eyes...? No, don't look...tell me...

Ladies, how many of you have asked the man in your life that very question and gotten the correct answer?

It's not that we don't love you. It's just... OK, OK, it's indefensible. You know the color of our eyes, why shouldn't we?

I can't explain it. It's not that it's unimportant. I know more than once I've become lost in a woman's eyes; men friends have confessed the same has happened to them. Another of life's mysteries; like not remembering your woman's birthday, unless it coincided with the date of the Super Bowl.

So women, how to proceed? Let's live in hope and continue to describe your eyes in the most alluring way.

Guys–just look in the mirror, so you at least get that right.

■ ■ ■

Do: Be consistent. Stick to one set of colored lens, and always check you haven't mixed and matched.

■ ■ ■

Don't: Answer question after you've peeled an onion.

■   ■   ■

Don't: Confuse terms. *Bloodshot is not a color.*

■   ■   ■

Don't: Boast *they light up a room!* In other words, you're a zealot?

■   ■   ■

Don't: Be lazy. If you can't tell without your glasses, put them on!

■   ■   ■

Don't: Write *Baby Blues.* Not an eye color when you subscribe to AARP.

■   ■   ■

Don't: Tout *ForYourEyesOnly* again! It was a real stretch to use it as your screen name, why remind her once more, you don't look at all like James Bond.

■   ■   ■

Don't: Imply as turquoise green as the waters off Anguilla. This is code for take me there every winter.

■   ■   ■

Don't: Make them look too hard. *They're the windows into my soul* might make him see something he doesn't like.

■   ■   ■

Don't: Promise *I only have eyes for you.* Nice thought, but he'll only think you're hiding something, that is, you have a glass eye.

■ ■ ■

Don't: Be transparent. *My best quality…really?* If you're going to continue dropping in bits of self-conscious braggadocio, can you be a little less obvious?

■ ■ ■

Absolutely Do Not: Rave about laser surgery. He'll laser in on making an appointment for himself and lose sight of your charms.

■ ■ ■

I wrote blue, but I have colored contact lens and switch them to match my mood.
Gloria, fifties, divorced twice

■ ■ ■

This seems to be one of the most useless questions. I'd be more interested in finding out how many women had glaucoma instead of having to meet them and then be forced to hear about their surgery. I guess that goes for men, but I don't think we complain about stuff like that as much as women.
Gavin, seventy-two, widower

■ ■ ■

Before I went online, I treated myself to an "eye-lid lift." I feel and look ten years younger. Gave me the confidence I needed to date again. So far, nothing serious, but plenty of prospects, so I'm encouraged. I'm not saying every woman

should go to those lengths or spend the money. I do say you need to do everything in your power to give yourself the confidence necessary.
BL, seventy-four, widower

■ ■ ■

Lifestyle

■ ■ ■

I want someone who can just make me laugh
and just be normal and understand my lifestyle
and how I want to live.

—SELENA GOMEZ

ARE YOU REALLY as good as you look? You heard me. *Are you really as good as you look?*

You're shaking your heads, aren't you? You're wondering what the heck am I talking about? Let me cue you in. What this section is all really about, what it's trying to discover in its own devious way is…exactly that!

Are you ready to prove it? Are you ready to come up with the right answers, so nothing in your daily routine, causes them to jump ship?

For instance, do you really want to let it slip out that you stay in bed until four, eating bonbons and doing your nails?

How about confessing you're addicted to three-hour competitive spinning classes except on the days you're doing hot yoga?

Then there's the ex-spouse showing up waving a skillet, demanding you return the wedding gifts her family purchased thirty years ago.

Finally, let's delete those so-called innocent lines about Tuscany that has every woman you meet trying to inveigle a summer invite. (Like you could afford a weekend at the Jersey Shore, let alone an Italian villa, without going broke?)

Follow my lead, and you can charm them into thinking you live a charmed life.

■ ■ ■

I did have thirty horses at one time…have a beautiful rescue dog from Katrina. Looking to share my love with another animal lover.
Donna, late fifties, divorced

■ ■ ■

Write me if you want to hear how the buckle of my Cambodian crocodile belt got stuck, and I had to call an emergency shoemaker to get me out of it.
Name withheld

■ ■ ■

I've been on the Internet for over five years, and for someone over fifty, it can't be beat, especially, if you live in Manhattan, like I do. I could go out every night of the week with a different woman. And I would, if I could afford it.
Steve, midsixties, widower

■ ■ ■

I'm shy, so I'd never go to a gay bar. Consequently, online dating has given me a second chance at finding a meaningful relationship. So far, I've not found that special someone, but I have made several new friends I never would have encountered for it not for this new social-networking phenomenon.
SA, fifties, single

■ ■ ■

Usually clad in New Balance walking shoes, sometimes shop in thrift shops for designer slacks with small fitted waists. I follow ideas wherever they take me and have written about my discoveries. I am currently contemplating more of the same once I get my bearings. I am independent. If intrigued, write me.
Gloria, fifties, divorced twice

■ ■ ■

I always pay for dinner. I never get upset when they're fifty pounds overweight or realize their pictures are ten years ago. What does piss me off is when they have the nerve to ask why I didn't wear socks when I'm wearing a suit. Don't they know we're in South Florida? Damn it, they're old enough to remember Don Johnson in "Miami Vice," right?
Gavin, seventy-two, widower

■　■　■

I'm a "player." I'm not interested in long-term relationships. Actually, I'm not interested in anything resembling a relationship. I'm strictly looking to date as many women as I can and having sex with each one. No, I don't actually come out and say that in my profile. If I did, I'd never get a date. At least not on Match, or any mainstream site like that. I can see you want to know why I'm not on a hookup site? The answer—not enough of a challenge. I like to charm the women into bed, and I'm not averse to working a little bit to get it done.
Cal, sixties, divorced twice

■　■　■

What's with men over sixty and athletic apparel? I'm fifty-nine and remember nobody over ten wore a baseball cap or team jacket unless on the ball field. Now you have every sport imaginable and teams from countries I never heard of. Plus events like the Super Bowl or the Olympics. You wouldn't believe how many guys show up on a first date wearing team caps, jackets. One guy said it shows allegiance. The worse is when they show up in cleats. Thank God, they were rubber and not metal. He said he liked the way it looked. I get it, they want to be kids again, but how'd they like it if I came with a jump rope and jacks?
Nan, fifty-nine, divorced

■　■　■

Your Marital Status

■ ■ ■

Be careful who you pretend to be.
You might forget who you are.

—ANONYMOUS

WOMEN I'VE INTERVIEWED think this category should be called, *No Place for Cheaters*. One vet who's been burnt, makes sure she gets the guy's address, so she can drive by his house to see whether he's living there with his wife or another woman. She also has a fondness for playing the Eagles tune, "Lyin' Eyes."

Men I've talked to voiced no such concerns. None demanded home phone numbers or called women late at night to see if another man answered. Certainly, none admitted to staking at the woman's house or following her during her daily routine. (OK, only one woman confessed she did that but that was only after she went through his clothes and found a wedding ring.)

I never discovered if men were more trusting or just didn't care. However, they did admire the woman who staked out the guy's house and wanted to meet her. I told them I was writing a book, not acting as a matchmaker.

■ ■ ■

Do: Be truthful. Provide superiority when you catch him lying.

■ ■ ■

Do: Get the definition straight. *On the make* isn't a marital status.

■　■　■

Don't: Write *wish I had been buried with him.* If you do, you'll wish you had.

■　■　■

Don't: Write *miserable,* because you think *misery loves company.*

■　■　■

Don't: Leave blank. Only one conclusion—and you won't want them to draw it.

■　■　■

Don't: Add...*black* after w*idow.*

■　■　■

Don't: Reply *maybe.* That's the same as saying you're a little pregnant.

■　■　■

Don't: Write o*nly in this world.* They'll think you're married to a space alien.

■　■　■

Do: Think down the road. Lie—you—him—bed—hubby—gun—*bang*!

■　■　■

Don't: Mark *married* and then add...I haven't drained all his assets yet. LOL.

■ ■ ■

Don't: Go into detail. No need to give him the wrong impression and write *acquitted* after *widowed*.

■ ■ ■

Don't: Proclaim *not in the eyes of God.* This is code for you better behave, because there'll always be someone watching.

■ ■ ■

Don't: Add numbers. I'm sure it wasn't all your fault, but writing *6* after *divorced*, gets him thinking...you'll make 'em—*7*.

■ ■ ■

Don't: Use metaphors. *Once burnt, twice warned* will only make him think you're a pyromaniac.

■ ■ ■

Don't: Write *three-time loser* when referring to past marriages, as this only marks you as a negative person.

■ ■ ■

Don't: Be cocky and proclaim *between husbands.* If you think marriage is like connecting flights, you'll miss your next one.

■ ■ ■

Don't: Declare *free at last, free at last!* You may want to express relief; he'll think you've just got out of jail for killing your ex.

■　■　■

Don't: Lament *it's a long story.* If she wanted to hear tales of woe, she'd be at a bar, not reading your profile.

■　■　■

Don't: Be snarky and ask: *Why do you think I'm in all black?* Not everyone knows the difference between mourning clothes and a fashion statement.

■　■　■

Don't: Add...*I have very high standards,* as this will call into question his receding hairline.

■　■　■

Don't: Ask if *common law* counts? This demonstrates a history of noncommitment.

■　■　■

Don't: Answer *only in the eyes of the law,* unless you want a relationship with an inmate.

■　■　■

Absolutely Do Not: Inquire *if siblings count.* This isn't the movie *Chinatown,* and you're not Faye Dunaway.

■　■　■

Men lie all the time, so why I can't. No need to mention I'm a three-time loser.
NCB, fifty-nine, divorced

■ ■ ■

I wear all black all the time and was actually, nicknamed The Black Widow by a man I spent time with for a while. I hope that was the reason.
CP, fifties, divorced

■ ■ ■

Dear (x). Seeing you're a retired psychoanalyst, I understand you could not resist using your professional skills to read into my profile and determine I will never have a normal relationship until I resolve my anger issues. My only reply…how come you didn't bill me?
JJH, early fifties, divorced

■ ■ ■

I'm divorcé twice, and figured that limits your chances, so I left out the "two." Putting it back in because women are using sites to check you out, and it's just going to mean more trouble for me on the backend.
LJL, seventies, divorced twice

■ ■ ■

I'm not writing separated. Saying divorced. If it's going someplace, I break it to them gently. So far, no problem, except for one woman who became upset because she just came out of a relationship where the guy pulled a fast one and told her he was "divorced" when he was still "married."
KH, sixties, separated

■ ■ ■

Do You Have Kids

■ ■ ■

I have over 1,500 children
and not one comes to visit me on a Sunday.

—MEL BROOKS, *2000 YEAR OLD MAN*

I DIDN'T THINK to give this question a second thought. I never considered it to be a deal-breaker, until I went looking for a suitable match and decided I wanted someone who had kids and understood, for better or worse, their place in the hierarchy of any forthcoming relationship.

Let's be honest here. I also wanted someone who'd be happy to hear me talk about my children because they'd be just as delighted as me to brag (and bitch) about their most precious possessions (probably the only thing we ever got right in our lives).

As long as we're on the subject of kids, I should bring up the problem of telling them you're on a dating site. For me, this was even more embarrassing than joining one.

Naturally, my first inclination was not to tell them. Recent political events made me understand the cover-up is always worse than the lie, so I immediately fessed up; and to my surprise, received only praise and support.

I discovered friends of both sexes shared my apprehension, but that was nothing compared to the shame and embarrassment when they discovered their children put them up on sites without their knowledge.

Kids...What can I say but leave you with the words of the comedian Red Buttons. "Never raise your hand to your kids. It leaves your groin unprotected."

■ ■ ■

Do: Answer truthfully. Like *bad pennies*, they always have a way of turning up.

■ ■ ■

Do: Remember they're still yours, even if they sued you to be emancipated, because you wouldn't let them sleep with their iPhones.

■ ■ ■

Do: Check your tax *records* in the event you've actually forgotten you have dependents.

■ ■ ■

Don't: Blame them on the weather. *Not everyone has sex every time it snows.*

■ ■ ■

Don't: Explain where they came from. You didn't tell the *Baby Daddy*, why tell this guy?

■ ■ ■

Don't: Leave blank. They'll think: *impotent, barren, a brood mare* or worse...*they live with you.*

■ ■ ■

Don't: Include kids from other marriages—even if they do love you more than your own.

■ ■ ■

Don't: Lament *No*, because they don't Skype. Just your luck, they'll show up at your engagement party.

■ ■ ■

Don't: Count orphans in distant lands. Code for you're using them as a *tax deduction*.

■ ■ ■

Don't: Hold a grudge. Bitching about stretch marks will put images in his head your tummy tucks won't erase.

■ ■ ■

Don't: Go existential. Adding…*those you wished you had* will only make him yearn for the women that got away.

■ ■ ■

Don't: Lament *I regret the day they were born*. This gives them the idea that someday, you might feel that way about them.

■ ■ ■

Don't: Go into detail. So you were hit by a car and in a coma during your childbearing years…He'll just think you're accident-prone.

■ ■ ■

Don't: Complain. Not the place to bitch about how unsuccessful you were in poisoning the neighbor's kids.

■ ■ ■

Don't: Make them guess. If it's *twelve*, don't write your favorite movie was *Cheaper by the Dozen*.

■　■　■

Absolutely Do Not: Mention sterilizing your ex-spouse or how China got it right with their *one-child one-family policy*.

■　■　■

My daughter put me on without telling me. I thought about killing her, but I love my granddaughter too much.
FC, fifty-nine, divorced

■　■　■

Never-married is a red flag because it usually means they've never had kids, and as a general rule, guys without 'em can't appreciate the fact I put my children and grandchildren before the new man in my life. Believe me, I know I've narrowed the field and cut a lot of nice guys out, but that's just the way it is.
Laura, late sixties, widow

■　■　■

I spend a lot of time with my grandchildren, so I want a man who has some of his own, knows how important they to our well-being. I've been around the block a few times, so I've come up with a little trick to see if a guy's BS-ing me or not. I tell him it's my grandson's birthday and would he meet me in the children's section of Barnes & Noble to help me pick out a book. That way I get to see if he really knows "Goodnight Moon" from the Man in the Moon. Now, the guy I want to tell you about, who shall go unnamed, is helping me look for books when two kids run by, screaming, "Harry Potter, Harry Potter"! Before you know it, one of them trips and nearly falls. It was then,

I saw the guy who said he loved kids, pull back his left foot. Can you believe that shit?
Gloria, fifty-five, widow

■ ■ ■

Want to know about kids? I have them and only looking for men who also have had them, so we each have an understanding of how important they are in our life. That said, I'm seeing this guy, and believe me he knows how to dress, so I have no problem meeting him for brunch. We're over on Madison, and afterward, he says let's take a walk over to see the windows at Barneys. Now, what women doesn't want to do that, or say no when he asks if I want to go in? Now comes the surprise. We wander by the cosmetic counter, and he wants my advice on what to buy his twenty-five-year-old-daughter. OK, I help him out, then it's upstairs to the Chanel Boutique, and before you know it, I've spent two hours helping him purchase a wardrobe for his precious Tiffany-Anne. You know what he says; he says I'm his personal shopper and wants me to go with him the next day to help him buy jewelry for his other daughter. I kid you not!
Laura, late sixties, widow

■ ■ ■

Do You Have Custody

■ ■ ■

Our 25-year-old son moved back home
with an eye toward socking away money to buy a condo.
We never bothered asking how long he'd planned to stay,
but I got a pretty good idea when I walked into his room
recently.
In the corner was a milk jug with a few coins in it
and a label that read 'Condo downpayment.'

—ANONYMOUS (ONLINE VETERAN)

AT FIRST, I thought this question didn't have anything to do with people my age. After all, wasn't it many moons ago we saw our children leave the house for good? What followed were the stories—jokes about them never writing, calling, and moving across the country only to be seen at holiday time, or god forbid, when somebody's dying.

Then a little voice whispered in my ear. *Eric—get real!*

Can you blame me for not wanting to face the harsh reality of an economy that forces adult kids to return home, creating all sorts of unexpected *custodial issues*?

This does not even address the blowback from our children going through divorces and showing up with or without kids of their own.

I can't pretend to solve all these issues, but I can provide a humorous spin, so you can complete this section with a smile on your face.

■ ■ ■

Do: Be clear. They are *self-supporting*! End of story

■ ■ ■

Do: Remember what I said, suing to become *emancipated*? Not the place here, either.

■ ■ ■

Don't: Use free association. *Custody = battle = Ex = killing the son-of-a-bitch with my bare hands.*

■ ■ ■

Don't: Bring the big fellow into it. After writing *no,* there isn't any reason to add...*thank God!*

■ ■ ■

Don't: Try to justify it. So they're on The Food Channel; if you love their cooking so much, buy them a restaurant, just get them out of your house.

■ ■ ■

Don't: Add...*only at holiday time.* Let him find out when it's too late that Thanksgiving and Christmas can last a season if the kids are out of work—*again.*

■ ■ ■

Don't: Write *they live with the bastard!* Readers let go of those who can't let go of their anger.

■ ■ ■

Don't: Boast *they're quiet as mice.* And twice as nice, right? Two feet or four, pests are pests.

■ ■ ■

Don't: Be negative. I repeat—this isn't the time to tell him you regret the day they were born.

■ ■ ■

Absolutely Do Not: Confuse *custody* with *in custody.* You'll be busted if you so much as breathe a word about them being jailed for the weed you brought back from Colorado.

■ ■ ■

Another dumb question! I've written websites asking them to remove questions not applicable to boomer, but no response.
Gavin, seventy-two, widower

■ ■ ■

I'm in my sixties and date only in my age range, so this question doesn't apply. However, that doesn't mean people have some pretty strange relationships with their adult kids. I had a dinner date with a high-powered stockbroker. Five minutes after being seated, he took out his cell, placed it in his lap, and begins texting. Every ten, maybe twenty minutes, he'd be texting. It became a real distraction, so I asked him, why he had to be so consumed by business that it was ruining our dinner. It wasn't the market, it was his thirty-year-old married daughter, and they were playing a game! Any time one saw a man wearing a belt and suspenders they'd text each other. They had been playing this game since she was a little girl. He started laughing, thought this was funny. I told him it was discourteous. He said he does it at the office and nobody says anything. Well—I was no

employee, and I wasn't going to take it. I said something very unladylike and left.
Chris, sixty-seven, divorced

■ ■ ■

Do You Want Kids

— ■ ■ ■ —

For everything there is a season,
and a time for every matter under heaven.

—ECCLESIASTES 3:1

I HAVE TO admit this question caused me to open that bottle of Classico Riserva 2003 I was saving for the time I met that *certain someone* online. Too bad for me, the wine and roses would have to wait. After a glass and some reflection, I was still baffled. Were they trying to trick me into admitting I've lost my virility? OK, I'm no spring chicken, but didn't Picasso produce sperm (I mean kids) into his nineties?

Were they trying to tell me, if I wanted kids I'd have to start dating girls the age of my original *alligator* polo shirts?

What about you? When was the last time you heard of a baby boomer giving birth to a child, unless you read it in the *National Enquirer* and it is something to do with aliens?

Oh, I wanted to write something clever like: *Are you f-ing out of your mind?* Cooler heads prevailed. I had a second glass of Chianti, kept a tight grip on my civility and just said *no. Thank you...Nancy Reagan.*

■ ■ ■

Do: Say *no*. Anytime you can show common sense is a plus.

■ ■ ■

Do: Say *yes*, if you want to be listed in the *Guinness World Records*.

■ ■ ■

Do: Declare *yes*, if you want a foolproof way of getting into his will.

■ ■ ■

Do: Write *yes*, if what you want most for your eighty-seventh birthday is a paternity suit.

■ ■ ■

Do: Say *yes*, if just you love getting a year's worth of free stuff, even if it's diapers and baby powder.

■ ■ ■

Don't: Mention *frozen eggs*. You might as well write you're *frigid*.

■ ■ ■

Don't: Mention Picasso, that is, you want to have children when you're ninety.

■ ■ ■

Don't: Confess *it's on your bucket list*. What biological clock are you watching?

■ ■ ■

Don't: Be a cradle robber and ask *why do you think I'm on this website*?

■ ■ ■

Don't: Use this space to talk about infertility. This is a dating site, not WebMD.

■ ■ ■

Don't: Think it's time to ask if your real children should now meet your love child?

■ ■ ■

Don't: Confess Viagra has you thinking differently about having kids. More code, more Picasso.

■ ■ ■

Don't: Reveal it's because God had other plans for you. And what might they be? No–I don't want to know, and sure as heck, neither do they.

■ ■ ■

Don't: Take the opportunity to talk about the mistakes you've made. Get it straight—no one likes a whiner.

■ ■ ■

Absolutely Do Not: Declare you would rather suck on nails than bring anyone from your gene pool into this world.

■ ■ ■

I take it back. The last question wasn't the dumbest, this one is!
Gavin, seventy-two, widower

■ ■ ■

At first I used to write something sarcastic, then I realized I might be offending women who perhaps wanted kids but weren't as lucky as me.
Jack, fifty-nine, widower

■　■　■

I'm confused. Why, must every dating site dedicated to our age group include the question: Are you planning to have more children? Are they nuts or just too lazy to realize how dumb that question is?
Donna, sixty-eight, divorced

■　■　■

Do You Smoke/Nonsmoker

■ ■ ■

Truth is, he loved me more than I loved myself.
So I sparred him and returned to my cigarettes.

—ANONYMOUS

A GOOD FRIEND put the question to me. You choke at the slightest hint of cigarette smoke, but when the most tantalizing woman sits down next to you at a bar smiles, introduces herself, and you get whiff of cigarette breath, what do you do?

Take one for the team? He liked that response. So did the other male interviewees.

Boomerettes were less sanguine. They were more than willing to leave at the first hint the guy was a smoker. One sounded like Sherlock Holmes saying, *the first thing she looks at are his fingers;* the slightest sign of a yellowish discoloration and she immediately knows he's not a dating material.

Then there are the women where age has dulled their olfactory senses to the point they can't tell Blue Cheese from Brie, but can miraculously sniff out the faintest whiff of five-day-old cigar smoke buried deep within the fabric of a guy's Harris Tweed jacket.

Go figure!

■ ■ ■

Do: Lie. You fooled your parents; you can fool this guy, too.

■ ■ ■

Do: Stretch it out. Like stretch marks, it's best revealed when you turn on the lights after you've made him feel sixteen again.

■ ■ ■

Don't: Mention Nicorette. Didn't I just tell you to lie?

■ ■ ■

Don't: Ask if cigars count? I'd wait until you discover they're addicted to brandy.

■ ■ ■

Don't: Ask if electronic ciggies count? A rose by any other name…

■ ■ ■

Don't: Do a Clinton. It doesn't matter if you don't inhale; it's everybody else who has to.

■ ■ ■

Don't: Go into detail. OK, not anymore, but don't add…a day doesn't go by where I don't think about toking on that fourteen-gram, four-skin beauty.

■ ■ ■

Don't: Brag only after sex. Why are you reading this book? Sounds like you already know how to get a guy—you vixen you!

■ ■ ■

Don't: Forget cops date, too. Saying your favorite song is "One Toke over the Line" will only land you a date with the judge.

■ ■ ■

Don't: Draw skull and bones. Reminding him of his own mortality only spells death for your relationship.

■ ■ ■

Don't: Refer to cigars and cigarettes as phallic substitutes. Remember, no comparisons!

■ ■ ■

Absolutely Do Not: Insert a smiley face emojis. Obviously, this is code for *you smoke' dem funny cigarettes.* (And no wink-winks either!)

■ ■ ■

I write I'm on the patch, and I want to avoid places where people smoke.
Steve, midsixties, widower

■ ■ ■

I love my cigars. Wish I could find a woman who doesn't mind their aroma.
Mel, fifties, divorced twice

■ ■ ■

The only thing I lie about. So far, been able to keep it going. Then again, not seeing anyone seriously.
Laura, late sixties, widow

■   ■   ■

A problem. I want to tell the truth, but pals tell me I won't get a response, even from women who smoke, because everyone's trying to quit.
Steve, midsixties, widower

■   ■   ■

I'd given it up, but smoke still lingered on my clothes, and if a friend hadn't told me to have them dry-cleaned, I'd have been in big trouble, because the first woman I met could smell it on guys three barstools away. Still dating her.
Hank, sixty, widower

■   ■   ■

Nobody answers this question truthfully, male or female. I've been at Happy Hour with friends who write in their profiles they don't smoke only to see them frequently duck out for a cigarette. As far as writing you're trying to quit, go into detail like you're on the patch/addicted to chewing gum, stuff like that, I don't see that in my friend's profiles either.
CP, fifties, divorced

■   ■   ■

I wrote I was trying to quit, and most of the gentlemen who contacted me told me the same. This was a problem for me, either way. If he was trying to quit, I guess we could do it together, but I ran the risk of one of us quitting and the other still smoking. Then there was the issue of I smoke, the guy doesn't...and me driving him nuts trying to quit. It was a lose-lose situation. In the end, I said no. I don't smoke. In the few dates I've had, nothing got serious, so I could

keep up appearances. I have no idea what's going to happen if I do find a man I want to see on a steady basis. Meanwhile, I'm down to two or three. I'm also thinking about hypnosis. One of my girlfriends tried it and it worked.
Donna, late fifties, divorced

■ ■ ■

Want to know how dumb my girlfriend is? She's an asthmatic and at our age that is very, very serious. My ex nearly died of it. Anyway, she sees this guy's picture, and he's on his yacht, smoking away on this huge cigar, and right away she falls in love. When she shows me the picture, I told her she's crazy. That all that smoking will get her sick and send her to the hospital. She says I'm the one who's nuts because smoke doesn't bother her when she's outside. Can you believe that? Like he's not going to smoke in the cabin? How about on land? You don't think he's going to smoke in his house or car? Come on? Anyway, she contacts him, and he's interested. Why not, she's gorgeous. Sixty-eight and looks fifty. Great work done and keeps in shape. She ends up in the hospital the first week she was with him. Got sick on board, and lucky they were just a few miles out of the harbor. Good story, huh?
Leslie, sixties, divorced

■ ■ ■

Your Drinking Habits

■ ■ ■

It provokes the desire,
but it takes away the performance.

—WILLIAM SHAKESPEARE, *MACBETH*

I FOUND THIS particular question hilarious. Then it dawned on me, as I stared at my second glass of Chianti Classico, I had been giggling for a while!

In vino veritas—my giggling was but a nervous indication I had to have liquid courage in order to sign up, or equally terrifying, continue my libation if I were to finish the process.

This awakening was followed by another revelation! I had to become sober and absolutely clearheaded if I was to fill out my profile in a completely truthful and honest way. And there was something else. Who knows what my drunken subconscious mind might blurt out? Yearning for a beauty that collected pornographic Hummel figurines, perhaps?

All I can say is, please follow my advice: *lose the giggles and fill out this section responsibly.*

■ ■ ■

Don't: Ask does beer count? Does the Pope live in Rome?

■ ■ ■

Don't: Promise to take up heavy drinking if they talk about golf at breakfast.

■　■　■

Don't: State the obvious and say: do you think I could go on a dating site sober?

■　■　■

Don't: Reveal your motto and say: drinking isn't a habit, it's a way of life.

■　■　■

Don't: Add anything about it being *a calming influence,* as this is code *for:* I can't handle you without being sloshed.

■　■　■

Don't: Say your favorite song is: "One for My Baby (and One More for the Road)."

■　■　■

Don't: Drop nicknames. It's fine your roommate remembers your college name, but let's face it; who else calls you: *Wooden Leg Lorraine?*

■　■　■

Don't: Be literal. When the choices are: *Sometimes, socially,* and o*n occasion,* don't answer, *all of the above.*

■　■　■

Don't: Begin with *only when I...*in other words, at the first sign of trouble, I'm six sheets to the wind, baby.

■　■　■

Don't: Mention *when flying all it takes is two drinks* and you see little creatures walking on the wing; and then you have to be subdued.

■　■　■

Don't: Brag. *So you can drink any ten men under the table!* Save it for when you crash his bachelor party.

■　■　■

Don't: Get the definition wrong. Writing *when the occasion arises* isn't the same as *occasionally.*

■　■　■

Don't: Blame others. Stuff like *I'm Irish what do you think,* just sounds like you hate your family.

■　■　■

Absolutely Do Not: Admit you are normally a quiet drunk, but when you realize you're in a relationship, you begin to sob uncontrollably.

■　■　■

I wrote socially. That covers a multitude of sins.
CP, fifties, divorced

■　■　■

A lot of my friends are just after a free drink. I don't think they have a drinking problem. They're just being ladies.
Nan, fifty-nine, divorced

■ ■ ■

I changed it from "special occasions" to "socially" when I realized that was the reason men weren't contacting me.
Chris, sixty-seven, divorced

■ ■ ■

I can't stand it when I write socially, and he thinks that means I want a glass of wine when we meet up for an afternoon coffee date. Coffee date mean that.
Helen, fifties, divorced

■ ■ ■

It's hard to tell if someone has a drinking problem or they just want to loosen you up so you'll have sex with them. I know I need a couple of cocktails if I'm particularly nervous, especially when I like the guy.
NCB, fifty-nine, divorced

■ ■ ■

Nobody is going to tell the truth here, especially when they like martinis. Especially when they're fifteen to twenty dollars, even at Happy Hour. At dinner, you can be spending twenty-five for some of the more exotic ones. At H. H. I'll pay for my own, but I expect him to pay for his, and if he wants a second, he's got to pay. On a date, he always pays.
CP, fifties, divorced

■ ■ ■

I'm not a drinker, but I wrote "socially," otherwise, you couldn't get anyone to contact you. I'll order a Campari and soda, and that will last me for the evening. I have friends who don't ordinarily drink, but because they want a second date with the guy, will match him drink for drink. I can't tell you how many times they've passed out or gotten so sick they could hardly make it to the ladies room.

CW, fifty, widow

■　■　■

If you write "socially" that covers a multitude of sins anywhere from one of my girlfriends who goes to sleep with a shaker of Martinis and wakes up to a cold beer. Funny thing, she hates Happy Hour and never drinks on a first date. On the other hand, my two best girlfriends and I go to at least three Happy Hours a week and nurse one Martini until someone buys us another, but never drink at home, alone, or anywhere else for that matter.

CP, fifties, divorced

■　■　■

Let's call her Nancy One. There were a lot of them up to Nancy Ten; anyway, this one was number one. We had a nice conversation online; agreed to meet for dinner. I'm not afraid to spend money because, I figure, half of it is for me 'cause I love to drink and eat, especially drink. We had a nice time. I took her to her car; we always agree to come in separate cars; and, because I'm a gentleman, I never try to kiss them, but reach out and shake their hands instead. Then I said I had a good time and looked forward to seeing her again. Guess what? She tells me that's the drink talking. Let me tell you, I know how to hold my liquor. What BS. You don't like me; tell me you don't like me.

Jack, fifty-nine, widower

■　■　■

Your Dietary Habits

■ ■ ■

All you need is love.
But a little chocolate now and then doesn't hurt.

—CHARLES M. SCHULZ

THIS MAY BE a tricky section if you weigh your dinner in a thimble instead of on a food scale, or have been known to say: just get me through the bedroom door and I'm yours.

Furthermore, no judgments if Gerber's is your solid food of choice, or you turn men on by taking a deep breath and bursting all your seams.

I'm just saying, if you're blushing, shaking your head, or giving me the three-finger salute, you might require my assistance more than ever.

Believe me, many a man has succumbed to the words *could I have fourths.*

■ ■ ■

Do: Open your fridge, as this will help you separate fact from fiction.

■ ■ ■

Do: Be considerate. I get it; you like to cook five-course meals, but did you ever think he might be on Weight Watchers?

■ ■ ■

Don't: Do movie quotes if they're vegans. "You like your liver with some fava beans and a nice Chianti." Really…!

■　■　■

Don't: Upset his Mamma. If you must put mayo on the Gefilte fish, make sure you tell him never when it's homemade.

■　■　■

Don't: Be out-of-touch. No meat on Friday? Don't you know in this country there's a separation between Church and Steak?

■　■　■

Don't: Confuse the issue. You cannot use dietary laws as a reason you have to have Dom Perignon with every meal.

■　■　■

Don't: Be biblical. Right, you don't eat birds that eat flesh or carrion, but could you just say you don't eat crow?

■　■　■

Don't: Be biblical. Sorry to refer back to the *Good Book,* but nowhere does it says that you're not allowed to eat in a diner.

■　■　■

Don't: Be totally honest. Sure, you love fasting because it allows you to see angels floating above your head, but save it until he can appreciate your idiosyncrasies.

■　■　■

Absolutely Do Not: Tout your peach cobbler as a religious experience, therefore, exempting it from the rules of Lent. *Joan of Arc was burned at the stake for less.*

■　■　■

Who's going to admit they're addicted to Krispy Kreme glazed donuts? *Come on, we all pretend we're healthy eaters.*
Nan, fifty-nine, divorced

■　■　■

Always a hoot when the fellow who says he's dieting asks we split a dish. Sure, I feel for him, think portion control is an important part of eating healthily, but when you invite a girl out on a date? Let's face it, cheap is cheap.
Helen, fifties, divorced

■　■　■

There are women who only want you to take them out to expensive restaurants and order the most expensive dishes on the menu. That's why I never let them pick the place. And if I get resistance, I say OK but cancel at the last minute.
Hank, sixty, widower

■　■　■

I like casual dining. Nothing fancy, low key, so I can get to know the gentlemen, and he can get to know me in a nonthreatening environment. So what do you think casual dining means to them, dress-wise? Unpressed chinos, wrinkled shirt half-in, half-out, and what's dumber than my ex's twenty-something bimbo...a baseball cap...on backward! I'm starting to see the over seventy-five-crowd wearing 'em sideways. I think it's a sign of Alzheimer's.
CP, fifty, divorced

■   ■   ■

I love to eat well and I don't mind taking a woman out to an expensive restaurant for an evening of fine dining. Let's face it—I like to eat, drink, and impress the hell out of them. Show I can afford it. There's only one problem. If she's a dud, I'm stuck, and no amount of filet mignon and an expensive burgundy can get me through two hours of listening to a woman bitch about the men who did her wrong or worst, the children who don't love her. Tell you the truth, I think it's only coffee dates from now on.
Mel, fifty, divorced twice

■   ■   ■

Your Religious Attendance

■ ■ ■

A good man, is a good man,
whether in this church, or out of it.

—Brigham Young

Do not read *The Da Vinci Code* before you fill this out, otherwise, you will fall under its spell, and instead of providing a simple, noncontroversial answer, you will go off into a stream of consciousness rant about religious conspiracies.

Fortunately, I had my coauthor friend check my answers before I submitted them and was saved the humiliation of being summarily rejected by the website as a hieratic.

One interviewee told me he had a coffee date with a woman who seemed fine, until she told him God spoke to her in a dream and promised her she'd find love with a redheaded man.

OK, he had only a wisp of red in his thinning hair, but at their age that was good enough; because she was extremely attractive he thought there was a God.

However, we all know, He works in mysterious ways, so it wasn't such a surprise when his date left him for the young barista with spiked hair, the color of a flaming sunset.

Makes you a believer, doesn't it?

■　■　■

Do: Know your initials. Want him to spend Sundays at services instead of watching the *NFL*? *Not **F**-'ing Likely!*

■ ■ ■

Don't: Reveal it's the only place you feel free enough to speak in tongues.

■ ■ ■

Don't: Blame others. Stop saying *the devil made me stay home.*

■ ■ ■

Don't: Confess that you need to be forgiven. You sound like a serial killer.

■ ■ ■

Don't: Answer between *my God and me.* In other words, you hear voices.

■ ■ ■

Don't: Brag that giving half your income to televangelists still leaves you quite well-off.

■ ■ ■

Don't: Elaborate. It's enough to say *at holiday time.* Don't mention the hundred candles you light each day for the saints you adore.

■ ■ ■

Don't: Answer *the Earth is my tabernacle, and I attend services every minute of my life.* Tell me, when will you have time for a poor soul like him?

■ ■ ■

Don't: Go off-topic, that is, this is not the place to admit you get your doll-making skills from the Haitian side of the family.

■ ■ ■

Don't: Mention family and reveal the person who wrote *The Exorcist* got the idea for the 360-degree head spin from your grandfather.

■ ■ ■

Absolutely Do Not: Be gullible. Doubtful you're going to find one of his faith that builds arks, parts seas, or takes down bullies with a slingshot.

■ ■ ■

I wrote in my profile I only attend services on the high holy days, but twice I got involved with guys who give me a hard time when the holidays come around, and I ask them to come with me. I have to figure out a way to add something in my profile that makes it clear that if we're in a relationship, we do things together.
Linda, sixties, widow

■ ■ ■

I know there are two things you are never supposed to talk about when dating a gentleman—religion and politics. Funny thing is, the subject never comes up when I'm dating blue-collar guys; you know, firemen, policemen, plumbers, guys who are supposed to be conservative and strict Catholics, right? Never happened with them, but it did came up with a stockbroker. We hadn't even finished our second cocktail when he told me that even if we didn't become a couple, he wanted me to convert to Catholicism. This must have been his thing, because he opened his phone and scrolled to a listing of the Catholic churches on the Eastside of New York. Then—can you believe—right at the table he e-mails the list to me! On top of that, he had videos of the Pope's visit to New York and he e-mails me them, too.

Laura, late sixties, widow

■　■　■

Your Activity Level

■ ■ ■

Do you believe in love at first set?
Or should I curl this barbell another 10 times?

—ANONYMOUS

WHEN I ASKED one dating vet what single piece of advice she would give to newbies, she said, "If you aren't active, get active and as fit as you can. Not only does it make you attractive to the opposite sex, it also increases your energy and confidence, two key ingredients to successful dating."

Well, what's good for the gander is good for the goose, so I figured can't hurt, especially since I was going on a date that evening and thought showing her a selfie of me doing wind sprints would be a great opening line.

I started off slowly on an oval path in my housing complex but was quickly overtaken by an octogenarian pair of *race walkers*. To their credit, they gave me a sorrowful glance as they kicked dirt in my face.

I know, I know—should have worn sunglasses, but as it turned out, they would have only fallen off and broke when I bent over to dry heave into the bushes.

■ ■ ■

Do: Take a few deep breaths, raise hands high, and touch your toes (maybe skip that), to give you the confidence you need to fill out these questions.

■ ■ ■

Do: Be positive. Don't lose the chance to show 'em you're up to the rigors of being arm candy in public and a whore in the bedroom.

■　■　■

Don't: Dare, challenge, or intimidate. Wooing isn't *loan sharking.*

■　■　■

Don't: Reply *not active at all,* that is, might as well forget *about sex in my lifetime.*

■　■　■

Don't: Post medical records. Not everyone can understand an EKG readout.

■　■　■

Don't: Tout speed walking. Who wants to be your next Dead Husband Walking?

■　■　■

Don't: Invite him for a day of competitive spinning, unless you want to see him spin out of sight.

■　■　■

Don't: List recent surgeries. Getting kneed in the family jewels by a titanium patella turns off the most ardent lover.

■　■　■

Don't: Cite the five marathons in five days on five continents. He can hear you saying *not tonight hon…I'm a little rundown.*

■ ■ ■

Don't: Boast about your genetics. The last thing he wants is to go jogging with you, your mom, grandma, and great-grandmother.

■ ■ ■

Don't: Boast how your facelift makes you look twenty-five. This isn't the movie *Chinatown,* and who cares if everyone thinks your daughter is your sister.

■ ■ ■

Don't: Be graphic. Terms like *viselike grip* will only make him afraid to shake your hand, that's if he's even brave enough to contact you.

■ ■ ■

Don't: Post marathon pics of your crossing the finish line. Call me old fashion; I don't like women who look like they haven't eaten in a year.

■ ■ ■

Don't: Talk mind over body, unless you differentiate between those who dig running over burning coals, and the whip and chain crowd.

■ ■ ■

Don't: Bring up the X games. Nobody's getting on the back of your bike and sailing over twenty parked cars as you do air wheelies on your BMX.

■ ■ ■

Don't: Extol the virtues of a run that takes all day. She's to do what...wait for you at the door with a silver cape in her hand?

■ ■ ■

Don't: Confess you never take off your running shoes. How romantic, drinking champagne out of a sneaker!

■ ■ ■

Do: Be smart. Sure, pulling a boat with your teeth across the bay turns some women on, but is it worth it at your age, and with your dentures?

■ ■ ■

Don't: Brag at the gym that you arm-wrestle guys to their knees, or you'll be the one screaming *Uncle, because you're not getting any e-mails!*

■ ■ ■

Don't: Cite the Ironman Event. Just the name makes me envision you bending steel bars with your bare teeth.

■ ■ ■

Don't: Think fitness apparel is eveningwear. Call me old fashion, but Lycra and a string of pearls just don't do it for me.

■ ■ ■

Absolutely Do Not: Talk about repelling off the Empire State Building. This is almost as repelling as dating Spider Woman.

■ ■ ■

Physical therapy to cure a bad knee, so I can walk, do as much yoga as I like.
KK, late fifties, widow

■　■　■

I haven't posted my picture yet. I'm 5'2", 120 lbs, physically fit, and I'm told, attractive. Maybe I'll hear from you?
C, sixty-nine, widow

■　■　■

I have also balanced my work with dancing, whether it is jazz classes or ball-room, specifically salsa and swing. Am in great physical shape.
Gloria, fifty-five, widow

■　■　■

One-time bungee-jumper—never again! Four-time marathon runner—many years ago; dog sledding in Canada—mush, mush!
NCB, fifty-nine, divorced

■　■　■

I am a high-energy person who exercises to keep in shape and to be healthy. I believe in growing old gracefully, and hopefully you have good genes.
Nan, fifty-nine, divorced

■　■　■

The gym has become a significant part of my routine. I do yoga and Pilates a few times a week and try to fit in cardio and weights, once or twice a week.
Karen P, late fifties, divorced

■　■　■

Will You Relocate

■ ■ ■

Come live with me and be my love,
And we will all the pleasures prove,
That valleys, groves, hills, and fields,
Woods, or steepy mountain yields.

—CHRISTOPHER MARLOWE

YOU KNOW THE saying, "Looking for love in all the wrong places"? This is what they mean when you answer yes in this section.

Just step away from the computer, take a few deep breaths, and then look out the window. What do you see: One of the world's best hospitals? The only hair salon that can color your hair so you look twenty-five again? The kind of excitement, vibrancy at all hours of the day and night, so you never feel alone?

Go into the kitchen and pull out the stack of take-out menus. Think you can find: chicken piccata from Franks in Chattanooga, sushi from Hanne in Sioux City, or veggie cream from Ess-a-Bagel in Virginia? (OK, I'm getting personal.)

Just remember, love can take you only so far when you're a baby boomer, except maybe Florida. (But that's another story, for another day.)

■ ■ ■

Do: Understand *relocation* has nothing to do with moving up in the world.

■ ■ ■

Don't: Proclaim *my bags are packed!* He'll think you live out of a suitcase.

■ ■ ■

Don't: Be political. Only guys in Red States means no ski house in Aspen.

■ ■ ■

Don't: Relive old history. No need to tell anyone your family was run out of the Ozarks because too many animals in the neighborhood went missing.

■ ■ ■

Don't: Overpromise. When you wrote *you love island hopping,* you were talking *Caribbean*—not *New Guinea.*

■ ■ ■

Don't: Write *wherever my heart takes me.* At your age, you should think motorized transportation.

■ ■ ■

Don't: Be confusing. *You—me—Shangri-La*…He'll think he's getting two for one, and won't be happy when only you show up.

■ ■ ■

Don't: Say you're looking for a man you can steal horses with, until you check his name against a criminal database.

■ ■ ■

Absolutely Do Not: Declare *been there, done that,* that is, I'm already in Witness Protection.

■ ■ ■

Just took my first cruise and thinking about taking one around the world. Will share expenses. Are you game?
Caroline, seventy-four, widow

■ ■ ■

Live in Paris but looking to return to New York after twenty years abroad. Your profile indicates you would be a perfect match.
Ava, fifties, single

■ ■ ■

There is an entire group of women here who are only looking for men up north so they can leave Boca during the summer months.
CP, fifties, divorced

■ ■ ■

I have a lovely home in South Beach but miss NYC. If you're willing to share your life with a snowbird, let me know, and we can have the best of both worlds.
FFF, sixty-five, widow

■ ■ ■

If you are willing to meet/date an outstanding lady from elsewhere who is open to relocation, please check out my bio. Interested? Please call, as I don't

do personal e-mails. If that goes well, you'll come out and meet me. I'm worth it!
Claire P, sixty, divorced

■　　■　　■

There was a woman who lived out-of-town, but she reached out to me because she said she was seriously thinking about relocating and was subletting a place in the city to see if she could swing it financially. I should have realized she was looking for someone to support her. It took two dates, but I got the message.
Steve F, sixties, widower

■　　■　　■

My Background

■ ■ ■

The best lies about me are the ones I told.

—Patrick Rothfuss, *The Name of the Wind*

I know the title sounds so very personal and intrusive, even a bit ominous to some of us. Face it—it's a little embarrassing to admit you've slept in the same bed as your older brother—until you were twenty.

What if the site's hacked and WikiLeaks posts your profile? Leaks the inconvenient truth...*he's still living with you*?

Then there's family. Not everyone has three or more blood relatives on *America's Most Wanted*.

Truth be told, we're more afraid of being alone than having our past revealed, so we cross our fingers and our toes, and hope the risk is worth it.

Not to worry, when you're finished answering all these questions, you'll even believe you were the family favorite, the class president, valedictorian, star athlete, and recipient of the Nobel Peace Prize. (OK, maybe not the peace prize...)

We'll put so much spin on it that he won't be able to see straight until he contacts you.

■ ■ ■

I recently traded the Rocky Mountains for the skyscrapers of NYC.
Melisa, sixties, widow

■ ■ ■

Have never been Miss Israel, Miss USA, Miss Universe or Miss New York, except in my heart and eyes of the men who have adored me.
LCF, sixties, divorced

■　■　■

Spirited, refined PhD psychologist, worldly life traveler with sparkling eyes, warm smile, petite, trim, fit, divorced, love to laugh and have fun, sense of adventure, intellectual curiosity, enjoys outdoors, classical music, jazz, visual and performing arts, reading, language. How's that for an opening?
LK, fifties, divorced

■　■　■

What works is recharging my batteries. On for six months, off for three, gives me perspective. Allows me to concentrate on live events. "Happy Hour," mixers run by dating professionals. I even put myself out by going to lectures, concerts. Never know who's going to sit in the seat next to you, right?
Donna, sixty-eight, divorced

■　■　■

Check out my profile, and write me if you like…Never been married but have had two long-term relationships, so I do commit. Always had dogs, boxers, and while you don't need to have any, if you do, we need to see how they get along as that relationship is just as important as ours. Always a city girl and want to stay that way. From your profile, looks like you share that view. Not to worry, have bathing suit, will travel to the beach during the summer.
FD, late forties, single

■　■　■

May have blurred the lines, but it's not like I was actually lying when I said I spend the winters in Boca and summers at the Jersey Shore. She certainly didn't have the right to have her attorney send me a letter saying, if I didn't pay her ten thousand dollars, she was going to sue me for fraud. Lucky my best friend's a lawyer, and after reviewing my profile and my relationship with this woman (I only exchanged a couple of e-mails), he told me she didn't have a case. Never realized there are sites that can dig into your entire life and come up with just about anything. All they need are your name, birthday. You know, the bitch even called my two sisters and threatened them? Now, I'm totally screwed because they won't invite to their places anymore.

Gavin, seventy-two, widower

■　■　■

Well, I'm looking for a man who is heavily tattooed with witty literary sayings up and down his arms and music notes on his back, so I can practice my two-part inventions on my fingertips. (Yes, just kidding, like you.) In short, down-to-earth, low maintenance, outdoorsy. Slender and in shape; love walking and hiking; travel often to exotic cultures to photograph people; and I have it all, except you. Looking for that wonderful ingredient of cuddling, handholding, exchanging serious and funny ideas that make life totally rewarding. And, you even look a little like William Hurt. What more can I ask?

VR, fifties, widow

■　■　■

Background, pretty ordinary? Online…now that's a different story. I'll call him Seymour. Nice face, interesting profile. We talked two, maybe three times before our first date at a wine bar. I knew right away he's not for me, but he's funny, and I'm a sucker for guys who make me laugh. We made another date for another wine bar. He called the next night, wanted to have phone sex. Like I said, background pretty ordinary, so naturally I've never had phone sex, but it's a new world, this Internet, so I'm not against it in theory. However, like I said, I wasn't interested in this guy. Another thing, I also don't like it that this sex stuff came out of the blue. Not one word in any of our previous conversations. I told him I'm not interested, but before I could hang up he said

he's already masturbating and suddenly he yells and said I made him hit the ceiling. I don't know what made me say it, but I told him they must be very low ceilings.
J, late fifties, widow divorced

■　■　■

Where Did You Grow Up

■ ■ ■

The landscape you grow up in speaks to you
in a way that nowhere else does.

—MOLLY PARKER

I KNOW THE first thing that comes into your mind is, *I've never grown up!* Well, you can forget that witty rejoinder and get down to it.

I lived in the same apartment until I was in my midtwenties. For many of my male friends, who grew up in the city and went to local colleges, this wasn't unusual. It was only later did I discover my life was highly unusual. Most of my new friends went away to school, and when they graduated, moved into their own place, often remaining in the same college community.

Then there was the group that, as young children, moved from town-to-town, city-to-city because their fathers' jobs took them there, or more dramatic issues faced them such as divorce or running away from bill collectors.

So while this question didn't faze me, I recognize it can pose a bit of a problem to others, therefore, my Dos and Don'ts are for you, and I hope they make you laugh and forget your own trials and tribulations.

■ ■ ■

Do: Change your accent. If you think New Orleans sounds more exciting and you're from Boston, better change how you say "park the car."

■ ■ ■

Don't: Answer *the Hood.* You didn't come *Straight out of Compton.*

■　■　■

Don't: Write *I moved around a lot.* This is code for being one step ahead of the law.

■　■　■

Don't: Namedrop. LA is just fine without adding *the chairman of the board "did it" in my bed.*

■　■　■

Don't: Be picturesque. No need to say *across the tracks.* (By the way, subways don't count!)

■　■　■

Don't: Be confusing. Unless they're into *Westerns, South of the Pecos* won't be much help.

■　■　■

Don't: Embellish. So you moved, no reason to boast you were the only one to get out alive.

■　■　■

Don't: Brag. Get real. It's not like *Canarsie is Paris, or Ralph Avenue the Champs-Élysées.*

■　■　■

Don't: List dimensions. *The house was so small the mice were hunchback* takes the romance out of it, don't you think?

■　■　■

Don't: Use latitude and longitude. They only want to know where you grew up; they're not planning a *National Geographic* expedition.

■　■　■

Don't: Be childish. *I'll never grow up…I'm Peter Pan?* Do you want to get the hook…from Captain Hook! (Remember, I warned you…)

■　■　■

Absolutely Do Not: Refer to home as a *workhouse*. You didn't grow up in nineteenth century London for God's sakes!

■　■　■

Thought Facebook was great for reconnecting with old boyfriends, but nothing beats this.
Ellyn, late fifties, divorced

■　■　■

She was from my old neighborhood, so when she contacted me saying she was living an hour away and wanted to reconnect, I got excited. She was always a looker. Her picture looked like she hadn't aged, and when she showed up heads turned. From her reaction, I thought she found me just as attractive. We had cocktails, dinner, spent three hours catching up, laughing ourselves silly. When we got to our cars, she kissed me on the cheeks. I get home, get a text saying she's

sorry, but there was never chemistry and that hasn't changed. I can't drive by the restaurant without thinking how I'd like to strangle her.
Steve, midsixties, widower

■ ■ ■

The trouble started when I told her my family never had an air conditioner until I was a teenager. Nobody from the neighbor did and it never seemed to bother us. During the day we went to the movies when it got really bad and at night hung out on our fire escape to catch a breeze. I told her that looking back at it, I only had good memories of those days. What really tore it for me was when she said, so you grew up in a slum? I was too much of a gentleman to give her a piece of my mind so I just laughed it off, made some excuse to get off the phone and never contacted her again.
Burt, seventy-four, widower

■ ■ ■

Can you believe, out of the blue, after sixty years, a boy who lived two floors above me for almost ten years sees my photo, remembers me, messages me? We had such a good time reminiscing. It brought back so many memories, some I had forgotten like how my father used to scream at his baby brother when he made such a racket running up and down the stairs that were right next to our apartment. Unfortunately, Tommy, that's his name, had just moved to the Virgin Islands to be with his sister and her family. So far we only Skype but who knows what might happen in the future? Great story, isn't it?
Terry, seventies, divorced

■ ■ ■

Your Ethnicity

■ ■ ■

Beneath the armor of skin/and/bone/and/mind
most of our colors are amazingly the same.

—ABERJNANI, *ELEMENTAL: THE POWER OF*
ILLUMINATED LOVE.

I THOUGHT THIS question politically incorrect and just left it blank. On the other hand, a foreign gentleman told me he came to New York because it is a city of immigrants, and he felt so emboldened to be a part of that environment, he felt comfortable revealing his identity on a site that reflected that admixture.

And here's another take. One friend got so ticked off by this question, she wrote, "We're all the same underneath the skin."

Being the wisenheimer that I am, I told her she should have written, "We're all the same underneath the sheets."

She threatened to purchase my book as a remainder! I guess she got the last laugh, huh!

■ ■ ■

Do: Refer to your birth certificate, not that you eat sushi seven days a week.

■ ■ ■

Do: Know your definitions. A…*Beyoncé* is not French for *"Soul Sisters."* B…*"Soul Sisters" is not one of the choices!*

■ ■ ■

Don't: Be defensive and declare, "If you prick us, do we not bleed?"

■ ■ ■

Don't: Go *au naturel* and say *the buzzards made me, and the sun hatched me.*

■ ■ ■

Don't: Write *Hebrew National.* Code for *you ain't kosher unless you like deli.*

■ ■ ■

Don't: Bring up the fact it's in your genes to eat your weight in food every day.

■ ■ ■

Don't: Mention *The Origin of Species.* Can you say, *"boring me to death?"*

■ ■ ■

Don't: Repeat what Maw said. No solid evidence *shrinking heads is in your blood.*

■ ■ ■

Don't: Declare unless it's *Homeland Security*, you find the question offensive.

■   ■   ■

Don't: Push it. *Social Media*? And your tribe is *LinkedIn*? Oh—and don't even think you can get away with *Blogger*.

■   ■   ■

Don't: Declare *member of the human race*. Only one step higher than we're all God's creatures, but just as sappy.

■   ■   ■

Don't: Be snarky. No, they can't tell from your picture. If anyone could, they wouldn't ask the question, would they?

■   ■   ■

Don't: Provide extraneous info. Just say *Asian;* no need to mention the family business or the cobra, the mongoose, the weekend exhibitions…

■   ■   ■

Absolutely Do Not: Write the name of the city where you were born. Duh!

■   ■   ■

I never contact anyone who leaves this blank or goes to the other extreme and talks about how God molded us all out of the same ball of clay.
Gloria, fifty-five, widow

■   ■   ■

As an Indian man, I wouldn't be in NYC, if I didn't want to embrace other cultures. I found this to be true for my straight friends who all agreed they chose dating sites that were multicultural.
SA, late fifties, single

■ ■ ■

I'm a black woman who's joined "white sites" and had only the nicest experiences, including several long-term relationships. In fact, been treated with more respect than on so-called "multi-racial sites" where men have been extremely critical.
Gail, early sixties, widow

■ ■ ■

He was Greek; I'm Greek. Not what I was looking for, but he made me feel comfortable. We even spoke it on the phone, just a few phrases, because I wasn't as fluent as Alex. So you have to believe how amazed I was when he looked me up on Ancestry.com, to see if my family was good enough for his.
Gloria, fifty-five, widow

■ ■ ■

Your Religion

■ ■ ■

My religion is very simple.
My religion is kindness.

—Dalai Lama

Oops, getting cold feet, are we? You're not really religious, but don't want to stray from the tribe for cultural reasons; now must decide to what extent you're going to lie to prove you're a card-carrying member. (I'm sorry, stretch the truth...)

Or—you may be a real risk-taker and resolve to join another tribe only to have last-minute jitters for fear the *God of Your People* will strike you dead for jumping ship.

Or—and this one is really perilous—you're an atheist or an agnostic, but are willing to throw away your belief system for a beguiling smile that sets your toes to tingle. (That's right guys get it, too.)

Not to worry Brothers and Sisters, you're sitting in the right pew, so just follow my advice, and like it says in Daniel 9:9: "The Lord our God is merciful and forgiving, even though we have rebelled against him."

(This is a message to my buddy, Craig. You do not woo women by quoting lines from *The Omen.)*

■ ■ ■

Do: Check *Wikipedia*. Hot Yoga is not a religion, no matter how popular it is with members of the clergy. (Same goes for Bingo!)

■ ■ ■

Do: Understand *Star Trek* was a TV show, and any of the religions depicted, no matter how attractive, aren't real.

■ ■ ■

Don't: Be snarky and write *God is Dog spelled backward*.

■ ■ ■

Don't: Say *the Devil* just because you listen to rock and roll religiously.

■ ■ ■

Don't: Proselytize. Bathing in the juice of agave plant may not float their ark.

■ ■ ■

Don't: Tell family secrets. It's nobody's business the entrance to hell is at Granny's basement door.

■ ■ ■

Don't: Talk about ceremonies until you show them how thrilling it is to throw someone off a cliff.

■ ■ ■

Don't: Write *umm*. Unless he's into Zen, he'll think "Umm delicious," and figure food is your religion.

■   ■   ■

Don't: Be a Luddite. Who sends cash in an envelope marked *To God in Heaven* when you can use *PayPal*?

■   ■   ■

Don't: Confess *you talk in tongues*. Men aren't great listeners to begin with, why make it even more difficult?

■   ■   ■

Don't: Confuse the spirit in the sky with the spirit world, that is, *there is no God called The Great Ouija Board*.

■   ■   ■

Don't: Say *Utah*. A state can't be a religion, even though having multiple wives is the answer to all your prayers.

■   ■   ■

Don't: Confess the flames coming out of the mouth of the stone God in your bedroom, isn't a fire hazard.

■   ■   ■

Don't: Mention *trances, angels,* or how exalting it is to leave your body and fly hand in hand with them around the room.

■   ■   ■

Don't: Use this space to complain about all the religious holidays that do away with alternative street parking and prevent you from getting a space.

■ ■ ■

Don't: Embellish. No need to write *Hallelujah! Hallelujah! Hallelujah!* You get them jumping out of their chair, maybe they fall and break their hip.

■ ■ ■

Absolutely Do Not: Use this forum to prove the existence of God by saying *your prayers were answered when the bastard was hit by a semi the day he left you for that teenage bimbo.*

■ ■ ■

I said I was Catholic and went onto a Jewish site because my first husband was Jewish and felt comfortable with Jewish men. Can you tell me why this one guy tells me, if I felt that way—why I shouldn't be wearing a St. Christopher medal?
Laura, late sixties, widow

■ ■ ■

I met a guy online, and we text, talked, until he asks me for a date the following Wednesday. I said it was Yom Kippur. He said he didn't know I was Jewish. I asked if that was a problem? He said no. He never contacted me after that. I guess it was a problem…for him…not for me.
Donna, sixty-eight, divorced

■ ■ ■

Many long, interesting phone calls in the last few months, but only two dates, both disturbing. Like clockwork, on the second date, each one groped my breast

when we hugged good-bye! I want a man with some class who can control his animal instincts. I am 27 percent Italian Catholic and 64 percent Jewish (Ancestry.com DNA)...both passionate cultures and religions. I am a loving, passionate, sensual woman...But please...be a man who understands the meaning of romance and foreplay.
Karen P, late fifties, divorced

■　■　■

We had a good conversation, decided to meet for dinner. During dinner we discussed religious beliefs. I know everyone says not to talk religion or politics, but I thought since we were getting along so well, that didn't apply here. I mentioned I was raised Roman Catholic, had a Jewish mother, studied Hinduism and Buddhism, as well as, Religious Science. I also mentioned the studies I have done on quantum physics. I thought he was impressed, but I read it wrong. When we next spoke, he admitted he thought I was a little "kooky," because of my comments about quantum physics. I tried to get him to elaborate, but he seemed to lose interest. We agreed we weren't right for each other. Just another guy who needs to do some exploration into the workings of the mind and the universe...or, one who isn't turned off by someone who has.
A, seventy-three, widow, divorced

■　■　■

The Languages You Speak

■ ■ ■

There are hundreds of languages around the world,
but a smile, speaks them all.

—Anonymous

As you can tell, I have a famous French name. Unfortunately, French was never spoken at home. I also don't have an ear for languages, so whatever college French I had, went in one ear, but did not come out my mouth in any recognizable form. This puts me in an awkward position when strangers begin *parlez vous-ing* with me.

I always felt alone in this insecurity until I met *L. Bonaparte and K. Verdi,* two Internet dates, who also did damage to their namesakes' native tongue.

We shared stories of mortification. We also laughed a lot, mostly at ourselves, but on the upside, came away feeling a lot more secure.

None of the online vets I spoke with gave this section much importance, although one male interviewee thought I provided him an opening and came back with, "What guy doesn't like a little foreign tongue?"

Off-color humor aside, regardless of what languages you speak, I'm hoping the language of love…speaks to you.

■ ■ ■

Do: Recite the pledge of allegiance out loud if at all confused as to your response.

■　■　■

Don't: Do dialects. *Yiddish will make him skittish.*

■　■　■

Don't: Answer *some.* That's one step below *broken.*

■　■　■

Don't: Try to impress. *Polyglot?* Oh, that will work…*not!*

■　■　■

Don't: Be trampy and answer *a little foreign tongue.* (See above.)

■　■　■

Don't: Reply *bilingual.* Guys have a hard enough time understanding women as it is, why double your trouble?

■　■　■

Don't: Be childish. *At's-whay up-way?* What's up? I'll tell you—no *pig Latin spoken here, buster!*

■　■　■

Don't: Answer in a foreign language. *Nein* to that; he's not dallying with a *Fräulein* in *Stuttgart.*

■ ■ ■

Don't: Brag. I'm glad you liked *The Miracle Worker* still no reason to tell him you're fluent in sign language.

■ ■ ■

Don't: Answer *multilingual.* Did you not see my warning about *bilingual, pitching Rosetta Stone, or another learning language program?*

■ ■ ■

Absolutely Do Not: Be Old-fashioned. *The language my fathers spoke? Really?* If they wanted to date your granny, they'd sign onto Ancestry.com.

■ ■ ■

He wrote Japanese, and all I could think of was Samurais lopping heads off.
Helen, fifties, divorced

■ ■ ■

I'm intimated when they speak three or four language, when I can't even ask where the bathroom is, when I travel. Keeps me from responding or reaching out to those really attractive women that keep popping up on the site.
Jack, fifties, widower

■ ■ ■

I am French and will come to New York in February. English is excellent. Speak Spanish as well as French. I will be happy to meet you.
Lisa, forties, divorced

■　■　■

The woman was French, and she reached out to me because of me having lived in France for three and half years and speaking French fluently. Sounds great, right? Although she had so many attractive qualities, something nagged at me, told me to watch out. My trepidations were soon borne out when she started to talk about how men only wanted to get between her legs and the numbers who had. Was she just insecure and bragging? A nymphomaniac, a hooker looking for new clients? When she showed me her apartment, the artwork, she confessed they had been gifts from admirers but now was trying to clean up her life and looking for a real relationship. Broke it off via e-mail. I just didn't know how right my instincts were.
Steve, midsixties, widower

■　■　■

Your Education

■ ■ ■

If you want to get laid, go to college.
If you want an education, go to the library.

—Frank Zappa

ONE OF MY online vets told me a story of connecting with a woman who happened to have attended the same college and coincidently, been in many of the same classes. They agreed to meet for coffee and catch up as they apparently had much to talk about.

What he hadn't anticipated was her reaching out to three college classmates she had kept in contact with, all of whom he dated during his school years, all of whom showed up for his coffee date. Needless to say, he no longer connects with anyone from his past.

Because I wrote a rather unorthodox essay, I hadn't the opportunity to specifically mention my educational background, nor any course of study. I thought the fact I attended film school would be a plus (make me more attractive), but my site only asked for levels of education.

After conducting a serious conversation with myself, I thought writing it in would be too obvious and probably be misconstrued by gorgeous young women believing I was a famous movie director who could make them a star.

I think you can see why the conversation with myself took over an hour.

■ ■ ■

Do: Be sly as a fox. If writing *some* is less threatening than *postgraduate in physics*–who's it going to hurt?

■　■　■

Don't: Ask if *street creds count*? If you got 'em, you know they do.

■　■　■

Don't: Be totally honest. No one needs to know Miami was your safe school.

■　■　■

Don't: List advanced degrees. Stuff like: *MSc, MBA,* and *LLM* makes them *run*.

■　■　■

Don't: Write *the School of Hard Knocks.* Strictly speaking, *you have a criminal record.*

■　■　■

Don't: Confess to being *twelve* when you entered college. This is about the age most boys learn to read.

■　■　■

Don't: Proclaim you're an autodidact. Nobody likes a braggart, especially one who can't just leave it at *self-taught.*

■　■　■

Don't: Brag you're the first person from *the mountain to go to college.* That's like admitting *Big Foot is your Daddy.*

■　■　■

Don't: List awards beyond *Milk Monitor.* Save *Valedictorian* and *Phi Beta Kappa* until you know he can spell them.

■　■　■

Don't: Cite the grades you skipped in grammar school. This only reminds him of being left back an equal number of times.

■　■　■

Don't: Tout a *Fine Arts background.* There's nothing *fine* about dragging him through a museum during the football season.

■　■　■

Don't: Go off-message. They're looking for your educational background, not how young you were when you learned the facts of life.

■　■　■

Don't: Reminisce. No reason to tell anyone that after reading the first chapter in *Introduction to Psychology* you had yourself committed.

■ ■ ■

Don't: Mention *Home Schooling.* That just makes them think you're narrow-minded when, in fact, you watch *Nature* and now believe the earth *is round.*

■ ■ ■

Absolutely Do Not: Go into detail. Your PhD is frightening enough, but adding the study of Jet Propulsion as it relates to the Theory of Relativity is relative to pointing a gun at his head and yelling run!

■ ■ ■

Never had time to finish college because I was drafted, so am going back to get a degree in philosophy.
Gavin, seventy-two, widower

■ ■ ■

The guy couldn't write a sentence. Spelling? The worst. I don't care if he's got a PhD; he wasn't going to hear from me.
Helen, fifties, divorced

■ ■ ■

I'm a dance teacher, but don't be intimidated. Will not expect you to be as professional, just show some proficiency. More important, a willingness to go dancing with me is essential.
Gloria, fifty-five, widow

■ ■ ■

The older I get, the more I want to return to the past, and one of my best times was at Michigan, so I find myself looking for women who went there or to a school where she had similar experiences.
Cal, fifties, divorced twice

■ ■ ■

Nothing turns me off more than when a woman's either is careless or just doesn't care like, when they check off all the answers: Master's Degree, JD/PhD/ Postdoctoral, Associate's Degree, Some College, Bachelor's Degree...
Jack, fifty-nine, widower

■ ■ ■

I went to NYU and have fond memories of my time there. This was reinforced by the fact I live close to the campus and find myself frequently walking around Washington Square Park. After my divorce, and at my sister's insistence, I joined a dating site, had a few coffee dates but nothing significant. Then one day I was walking around the park when a man my age catches my eye. He looks familiar. After a few awkward seconds we realize we've seen each other's photo on our dating sites. We go to coffee, and it turns out we were both at NYU in the sixties. I tell anyone who asks, online dating brought me my new gentleman...sort of...and it can do the same for you.
HG, seventy-four, widow

■ ■ ■

When I was in graduate school, I had a roommate who was taking a math course that worked like the card game Hearts: on periodic exams were one hundred true/false questions that if you could get all of them wrong, you would get double points. Your profile is a little like that, and I think I passed. I like the humor (even though you're not smiling in your photo). I guess, since you're an author, it's a good thing you write so well, as it was a pleasure to read. I'm afraid mine is kinda boring in comparison, but I hoped to make it informative

enough guys would know what they were getting. What do you think: should I say that I'm thinking of writing a book called "Finding Your Inner Bitch?"
Ellyn, late fifties, divorced

■   ■   ■

Your Course of Study

■ ■ ■

*I have never let my schooling
interfere with my education.*

—Mark Twain

To quote my favorite Olive Oil importer, "Just when I thought I was out they pull me back in." I mentioned Film School in the last section. What I didn't add is that it's a bit of a bitter memory. While several of my classmates have gone on to win multiple Oscars and become household names, I was never been able to break into the industry and become a director.

My conundrum: Do I dwell on the negativity or, perhaps, use it in a more positive, image-enhancing way?

If you're facing the same dilemma, let me tell you I decided to follow my own advice and lighten the hell up. I'd tell the one about how a student teacher taught me to load 16 mm film into an Arriflex by using a black bag to avoid exposure to light; how he became so frustrated by my lack of dexterity that he almost motioned an actor friend to come over and help. So what if they thought I knew Robert De Niro and could get them into the next Martin Scorsese movie?

■ ■ ■

Do: Check your transcripts. Just because you know who's buried in Grant's Tomb doesn't deny the fact you majored in anthropology, not archeology.

■ ■ ■

Don't: List any *ologies: Zoology, paleontology*—it's all Greek to him.

■ ■ ■

Don't: List adult classes. Origami? He'll think you'll show up in a kimono.

■ ■ ■

Don't: List postgraduate courses. Please remember, inferiority is the sincerest form of flattery.

■ ■ ■

Don't: Go *foreign. London School of Economics*—speak *American*—say *bookkeeping!*

■ ■ ■

Don't: List *agriculture.* Unless you're the *farmer's daughter,* he'll think you just fell off the turnip truck.

■ ■ ■

Don't: List *life sciences.* Like *new age music,* he won't know what the hell it is and look for a new life with someone else.

■ ■ ■

Don't: Put on airs. It's enough to say *Harvard* without adding, *The Kennedy School of Government,* don't you think? Duh!

■ ■ ■

Don't: List *economics*. Unless it's *Home Ec*, it's code for *she knows more about how to control your money than you'll ever know.*

■　■　■

Don't: Count *the black arts*. The slightest hint *you can turn him into a toad* when he becomes uppity will cause him to up and run.

■　■　■

Don't: Embellish. *Social work* is fine but adding…leading to a degree in a Trauma-Informed Social Work Practice, will traumatize them.

■　■　■

Don't: Be a smart-alecky. *Study—I never cracked a book to get an A!* He hated those kids back in the day, so how do you think he's going to feel about you?

■　■　■

Don't: *Really* Embellish. It was as if Freud was teaching the course. Please— it was *Psych 101*, and the teaching instructor had a little goatee and a slight accent.

■　■　■

Absolutely Do Not: List *Women's Studies*. You might as well list *necromancy*; it's just as frightening to most men and just as much of a turn-off.

■　■　■

No joke. She wrote "linguistics," and I got tongue-tied!
Jack, fifty-nine, widower

■ ■ ■

MA, PhD in social work, and looking for gentlemen with equal appreciation for the needs of others. I put myself out there; don't you think you can do the same?
CW, fifties, widow

■ ■ ■

I have never had a problem with being truthful. I realize when I write I have advanced degrees in chemical engineering I made sure to add I have a wide variety of interests… sports, the arts and music. It is important for women to understand I'm a normal, approachable guy that is easy to be with. It also helps when I explain that for forty years I was in product development for a Fortune Five Hundred Company and was responsible for creating many recognizable household products.
Lester, seventies, widower

■ ■ ■

Your Occupational Description

———■ ■ ■———

No man has a good enough memory
to be a successful liar.

—Abraham Lincoln

OK, some male boomers still work, or are self-employed, but most are retired, so they jump at the opportunity to fulfill their lifelong ambition and *bullshit!*

No, you weren't a f-ing CEO, CFO, or COO!

Why shouldn't you exaggerate? I'll tell you why. First off, the less savvy, more greedy will immediately target you as a *sugar daddy,* and you'd better come up with the oodles of cabbage or, be outed for the four-flusher you are.

The number two reason—the smart ones will immediately check you out on the myriad of websites designed to polygraph your life and discover the minutest of secrets that years ago your former wives could only access by spending thousands on their own private eyes.

For some reason, most women don't need to bullshit. *Their downfall seems to lie in the opposite direction.* Too much honesty can be brutal, especially, when it comes to telling men you and your reading group, play the market and last year made enough money to sail around the world on the *Queen Mary 2.*

Here are some useful hints that, while they can't help you on the high seas, they can navigate you through the rocky waters of this section.

■　■　■

Do: Realize *clipping coupons* and *cashing alimony payments* aren't jobs.

■　■　■

Do: Check bank statements to dispel any doubts you are a *jack of all trade and master of none.*

■　■　■

Don't: Say *Export/Imports.* Code for *you smoke Havana cigars.*

■　■　■

Don't: Threaten his *masculinity* and instead of *construction*—say *home design.*

■　■　■

Don't: Call yourself *The Boss,* or you'll be *dancing in the dark*—alone!

■　■　■

Don't: Use the term *professional,* when putting it in front of...*kickboxer.*

■　■　■

Don't: List it if you have to add disclaimers like: *former, reformed, or never convicted.*

■　■　■

Don't: Say *self-employed.* Same as *I work from home,* both code for *unemployed.*

■　■　■

Don't: Make him reach for a bottle instead of you by saying you *worked in a coal mine when you were six.*

■ ■ ■

Don't: List *mercenary,* unless you add *domestic only*; otherwise, she'll think you won't be home for dinner.

■ ■ ■

Don't: Resolve your anger. *Broodmare* might be appropriate, but it's best to be more upbeat and write *Mom.*

■ ■ ■

Don't: Be irrational. Why would anyone who's the *CEO of a Fortune 500 Company* be on a dating site?

■ ■ ■

Don't: Say *matriarch or patriarch.* (I can't even write the words without shaking in my boots, so what can you expect them to do?)

■ ■ ■

Don't: Make her wait. You think assuring her you'll come clean once she signs *The Official Secrets Act* will keep her from clicking off?

■ ■ ■

Don't: Say *Telecommunications.* We're so sick and tired of robocalls, even if you're the CEO of Verizon, you'll be tarred with the same brush.

■ ■ ■

Don't: Be too specific. Chef is enough. Adding anything about *sharp instruments* gives the impression you'd slice heads off at the first disagreement.

■　■　■

Absolutely Do Not: Make them guess. *Over five hundred customers served?* (Let me take a crack at it—running a Bakery—escort—drug dealer?)

■　■　■

I wrote CEO. And I'm proud of it.
LS, sixties, widow

■　■　■

I wrote Dance Teacher, and several guys contacted me to know what I would charge for private lessons.
Sally, seventies, divorced

■　■　■

I don't get it. They tell me what they studied, the degree they received, and then for occupation description write "other."
Steve, sixties, divorced

■　■　■

She wrote she taught English as a Second Language as well as Chinese and all the romance languages. Sure I was impressed, but at the same time couldn't get over feeling intimidated.
Gavin, seventy-two, widower

■　■　■

She wrote "psychotherapist" for occupation, but "other" for her "occupation description." I wanted to ask why, but was afraid she would think I was crazy.
Hank, sixties, widower

■ ■ ■

"I am a portrait photographer and have a secluded studio facing the water in Amagansett." He should have added: only models need apply. Come on, how obvious can you get?
GGG, sixty-five, widow

■ ■ ■

I wrote "Psychoanalyst" and received all sorts of vile messages addressed to "headshrinker" and "quack." At first I responded, defended myself and my profession, until I realized it was causing me too much anxiety. I now write "Healthcare professional" and no longer receive unsavory messages.
LLK, sixties, divorced

■ ■ ■

It does concern me when they don't write anything in their essay about what they did for a living. Some of the women I've dated tell me they're ashamed they were housewives or stay-at-home moms. Some told me they were embarrassed they were a part of a generation of married women who lived the lives of kept women or trophy wives.
BL, seventy-four, widower

■ ■ ■

Your Occupation

—■ ■ ■—

Never brag, never bluster, never blush.

—ROBERT BROWNING, *DRAMATIS PERSONAE*

NO—THIS IS not a misprint. It's also true, *Your Occupation* and the last category, *Your Occupation Description,* appear not only to be the same, but in reverse order.

Actually, this apparent duplication may be a blessing in disguise if, for some reason, you let anger and frustration (perhaps, even the bitter truth) get the better of you.

For instance, for *Your Occupation* you answered, *"Self-employed copywriter"* and for *Your Occupational Description, "Busy all day tearing up rejection letters from no-talent, inexperienced motherfuckers who think anyone over twenty-five should be on social security."*

So—let's return to the previous section to make certain you haven't strayed from your original portrayal as the exceptionally seasoned professional and not one who is boiling over with rage and recriminations.

Unfortunately, this bit of advice comes too late to a friend who was unable to check his *snarky* at the door and wrote, "What are you a moron? I just told you!"

■ ■ ■

Do: Understand the difference between *profession* and *professional* when it comes to c*lipping coupons* or *cashing alimony payments.*

■ ■ ■

Don't: Use euphemisms. *Between jobs*–that is, *out of work.* (Or, more unkindly, *unemployable.*)

■ ■ ■

Don't: Degrade his mother. *You served your time?* Would it kill you to say— something more positive like, *Stay-at-Home Mom?*

■ ■ ■

Don't: Make them feel worthless. OK, after practicing law you became a doctor but did you have to add...*then an astronaut?*

■ ■ ■

Don't: Use the term *entrepreneur.* OK, *substance man* is more enlightened, but still believes *certain job titles, especially ones in French mean: MEN ONLY!*

■ ■ ■

Don't: Use an acronym. *CEO, COO, CFO* is the apex of intimidation! You might as well pose between *Bill Gates and Warren Buffet.*

■ ■ ■

Don't': Go overboard. Attorney, OK. *CNN Justice Reporter*—give me a break!

■ ■ ■

Don't: Confuse vocation with avocation. *Following George Clooney until you get him to sign an autograph is not an occupation!*

■ ■ ■

Don't: Put on airs. Unless you want to cook gourmet meal every night, leave it at *Chef* rather than adding...*recipient of Michelin's four-star rating.*

■ ■ ■

Don't: Say *Activist. Second warning!* Even if picketing for a green garden occupies all your time...*it will be misinterpreted a bomb-throwing bitch!*

■ ■ ■

Don't: Be trampy. Come on *Masseuse!* Lie if you have to, but tone it down and go with *Physical Therapist.*

■ ■ ■

Don't: Be coy. *This and that...*That's your response? You know theirs? *Fahgettaboudit!*

■ ■ ■

Absolutely Do Not: Tell the truth. *Predatory Lender...*instead of banker!

■ ■ ■

Nobody is interested in what a chemical engineer does, so I left it blank.
Steve, sixties, divorced

■   ■   ■

Decided no man wanted a woman who wrote poetry: wrote "will tell you later."
NCB, fifty-nine, divorced

■   ■   ■

Wrote retired naval captain. Works great for me. Helps I have a boat and live in the Keys.
Mel, fifty, divorced twice

■   ■   ■

College professor. Got the occasional women asking if I could help get their grandchildren in college.
FRL, sixties, divorced

■   ■   ■

"I would love to cook for you, clean for you, and do those little things that matters the most." I didn't contact her because I don't believe in miracles.
Steve, midsixties, widower

■   ■   ■

Retired law enforcement, perhaps why I get to the point and wrote: "Not looking for friends, and I didn't join this site for pen pals or to improve my typing skills."
BL, seventy-four, widower

■   ■   ■

Use to be advertising, but after the hit show, I wrote Mad Man. Increased the amount of messages tenfold. Whenever I messaged them, always got a reply. Better than catnip.

Jack, fifty-nine, widower

■ ■ ■

I answered high school history teacher for twenty-eight years, and I cannot tell you how many guys compliment me on that and want to meet me because they have such fond memories of their female teachers.

Donna, sixty-eight, divorced

■ ■ ■

I wrote retired college professor, and all my friends told me I'd never get a man to respond and should simply write "teacher." They were wrong. No love of my life yet, but plenty of dates. My advice? Be truthful, let the chips fall where they may, and don't underestimate the Male Species.

Terry, seventies, divorced

■ ■ ■

I'm a retired attorney who does some pro bono work and wrote Law / Legal / Judiciary, and believe it or not, have had men write to ask how they can get out of parking tickets or DWI violations. I've also had some fan mail from male attorneys who just want to reminisce. Unfortunately, I have received a good deal of hate mail from men who felt the legal system did them an injustice during their divorce proceedings. This has led me to add to my occupational description that I do not handle divorce cases.

Laura, late sixties, widow

■ ■ ■

Your Income Level

■ ■ ■

You can be young without money
but you can't be old without it.

—TENNESSEE WILLIAMS

GUYS—THE BEST advice I got from an online vet was, "There is no romance without finance!"

Sad words but true, and for many men on a fixed income, this prevents them from going online and finding love.

The more unscrupulous pretend they're loaded, but in reality they must make a choice between buying their dates that second thirteen-dollar martini or stiffing the valet. Men in this position look for a woman, better known as a *purse,* to support them.

Women can be just as predatory, even more deadly. One interviewee swore she knew of at least two *Black Widows* at her golf club who got away with killing their husbands for money. She confided, "The cops may be stupid, but your hairdresser always know...and always can't keep a secret."

One, well-healed gentlemen bragged, "If you got it, flaunt it!" These were his *Golden Years,* so he went on, "Gonna show the gold—baby—show the gold!"

He added, he didn't care if they called him a cradle robber behind his back. "They were green with envy, because they don't have the green!" he shouted as he concluded our talk.

For the rest of us, I think it's best not to divulge your income until you're certain there will be a solid relationship in your future. (Can you spell prenup?) As I may have mentioned, I'm not above telling a little white lie, so if you must, I give you permission to write *will tell you later* without really meaning it.

This topic is no laughing matter, but I have to get you to lighten up, so here are my next set of Dos and Don'ts that will put a little humor back into your life.

■   ■   ■

Do: Write *will tell you later*. Always good to hold out hope, especially when you know once they sign the prenup, there won't be any.

■   ■   ■

Do: Act your age. *None of your beeswax?* Gee whiz, they'll think they're dealing with a child!

■   ■   ■

Don't: Write *$100,000* unless you want to be somebody's *purse.*

■   ■   ■

Don't: Be combative and say *you show me yours, I'll show you mine.*

■   ■   ■

Don't: Mention *income inequality.* That's code for *I want what's theirs.*

■   ■   ■

Don't: Choose *under* $10,000. If true, you should be out looking for a job!

■   ■   ■

Don't: Confuse them. *Sheltered or unsheltered?* They'll think you're selling real estate.

■　■　■

Don't: Be snippy and say *and I earned every penny,* that is, *and I'll never let you forget it, either!*

■　■　■

Don't: Be naïve. Come on—everyone knows you don't include money hidden in offshore accounts.

■　■　■

Don't: Write *over* $500,000. Now we're going beyond *the purse* and into *their winning lottery ticket.*

■　■　■

Don't: Leave blank. They'll think you have such little regard for money you won't even answer the question.

■　■　■

Don't: Take them for granted. Not everybody knows who's on *Forbes* list of the richest men/women in the world.

■　■　■

Don't: Challenge their math skills. Asking *dollars or Euros* will not endear you to anyone who has trouble making change.

■　■　■

Don't: Rail against the IRS. Remember, not the forum for bitterness, nor do you want to remind them how much they owe.

■   ■   ■

Don't: Write *the 1 percent of the 1 percent,* unless you want a 1 percent chance of finding anyone who loves you for you.

■   ■   ■

Don't: Make them jump through hoops. Saying, *you'll have to talk to my Swiss Banker* will only make them think twice, unless they have Vonage.

■   ■   ■

Don't: Ask if *trust funds count.* It will make them resent their parents for not being born with a silver spoon in their mouth.

■   ■   ■

Absolutely Do Not: Write *I stopped counting when I reached a billion.*

■   ■   ■

A fool and his money are soon parted. Leave this one blank!
Helen, fifties, divorced

■   ■   ■

"Will tell you later" means not until I trust you. Otherwise, you're on the Six-O'Clock News as another victim of a smooth talking con man.
GGG, sixty-five, widow

■   ■   ■

I learned from my first marriage that I couldn't count on anyone but me. That lesson served me well. I have a good job, saved my money, can take care of my kids. Those changes made me a lot more secure; made me appear independent, that's why I only attract like-minded men online and no scammers.
Chris, sixty-seven, divorced

■ ■ ■

The best advice I received was to write, "will tell you later" or even leave it blank. Also, never to reveal your income until you are getting serious with the person and are confident they aren't there for your money. I've heard too many stories of people conned out of their money not to take this advice seriously.
Ellyn, late fifties, divorced

■ ■ ■

I'm not a rich guy and learned the hard way when a woman says she travels a lot and expect her mate to accompany her; either she wants him to pay or split the costs. For me, neither works so, if you're like me, my advice—don't even waste time by replying, no matter how attractive, or how hot she is for you.
Hank, sixties, widower

■ ■ ■

Your Political Orientation

— ■ ■ ■ —

They say politics makes strange bedfellows.
I say arguing about it makes for an empty bed.

—THE AUTHOR

A MALE FRIEND lamented how he thought he had finally found the woman of his dreams, but it never came to pass. They had shared the same liberal point of view; however, because not every single topic came up, he had been blindsided when she refused to vote during the last national election, because no candidate promised to arm Greenpeace with missiles so they could destroy any ship that posed a threat to the whales.

I've never given up my principles, although, one time I put myself through some very intensive soul searching when an extremely attractive women, who wanted to live in New York during the winter months, offered to share her life with a *certain someone* on her sprawling plantation during the summer season. Fortunately, I was spared when I realized her annual *North Carolina Seceding from the Union Lawn Party* took place on the same day as the Coney Island Mermaid Parade.

■ ■ ■

Do: Be truthful. *Demes' you do, Demes' you don't.* Bite the bullet and lose those Republicans now or never.

■ ■ ■

172

Don't: Say *leaning to*...They'll only think you have bad posture.

■　■　■

Don't: Declare *I'm a lifelong*...in other words, you're *Daddy's Girl.*

■　■　■

Don't: Declare you're a *Liberal*, in other words, you're a *spendthrift.*

■　■　■

Don't: Be *trampy.* Come on—we all know what *swing voter* really means.

■　■　■

Don't: Be an *Anglophile.* OK, you love everything British, but that doesn't give you a reason to write *Tory.*

■　■　■

Don't: Write *Agitator!* Strictly speaking, same as *Activist*; both code for *one who doesn't take shit from any man.*

■　■　■

Don't: Write *will tell you later.* That's code for *Anarchist.* (Didn't I tell you he'd think the worst?)

■　■　■

Don't: Reply *Social Democrat.* You see how much trouble it caused *Bernie;* imagine what it will do to you?

■　■　■

Don't: Say *depends on who's running.* Demonstrates a lack of loyalty, and they'll think you'll cheat on them if someone better comes along.

■　■　■

Don't: Brag. So you became a *fiscal conservative* when you were *treasurer of your fifth grade class. La-de-da…la-de-da…*

■　■　■

Absolutely Do Not: Write *Pariah.* So you're a *Dem* in a *Red State…*They'll just mistake it for a disease, and you'll become an outcast here, as well.

■　■　■

Born and raised in a Blue State. Need I say more?
Ellyn, late fifties, divorced

■　■　■

This wasn't an issue, but after the recent election, it is now!
Helen, fifties, divorced

■　■　■

I always check to see if their politics agree with mine. If not, it's a nonstarter. If they've left it blank, I make sure to ask the first time I message them.
Jack, fifty-nine, widower

■ ■ ■

Liberal on social issues, conservative when it comes to money. No politics except with these ground rules: anyone stops listening, interrupts, I leave.
Steve, sixty, divorced

■ ■ ■

When he showed up wearing a "Make America Great Hat" after I made a big deal about voting for Hillary, I knew it was a nonstarter.
Helen, fifties, divorced

■ ■ ■

Your Zodiac Sign

■ ■ ■

It is not in the stars to hold our destiny
but in ourselves; we are underlings.

—WILLIAM SHAKESPEARE, *JULIUS CAESAR*

MEN—DO NOT take this question lightly. Above all, please be respectful. How would you like it if somebody told you the NFL is a pile of dog poop?

And no quips like, *who needs astrology? The wise man gets by on fortune cookies.*

I sure as hell would like to be as clever as Edward Albee, but because most women I know follow their horoscopes the way men follow the box scores of their favorite sports team, that would almost be as worse as never complimenting them on their shoes.

So—this is what you must do. Go onto Google and learn as much as you can about astrology. Then find your sign (it corresponds with the month you were born, duh!) and memorize its attributes. You now will be armed and dangerous, so, when you meet a woman who gushes over you being a Libra, you will show equal enthusiasm for her being a Scorpio. Suddenly, the stars in the heavens and the ones in her eyes will align and shine on you and only you.

Ladies—I'm preaching to the choir when I tell you how important his sign is to a lasting relationship. You've been checking out your horoscope in every magazine and newspaper since you saw your mom burst into tears when she discovered your father's real birthday.

■ ■ ■

Do: Understand that *Easy* is not an astrological sign.

■   ■   ■

Don't: Get her birthstone wrong. Duh!

■   ■   ■

Don't: Talk about *birthstones*. That's code for *take me to Tiffany's*.

■   ■   ■

Don't: Play *Devil's Advocate*. *666* isn't on any chart made in heaven.

■   ■   ■

Don't: Be a *Purse. Three planets in your house of money*—come on now.

■   ■   ■

Don't: Embellish. So you're a *Triple Leo*; no need to add…"*Hear me roar!*"

■   ■   ■

Don't: Declare at your last reading you were told, *you have sheep in your house of sex.*

■   ■   ■

Don't: Take this opportunity to tell him how seeing *Hair* one hundred twenty times changed your life forever.

■   ■   ■

Don't: Be trampy and say *The House of the Rising Sun*. Unless he's used to paying for it, you'll pay dearly when he clicks off.

■ ■ ■

Don't: Be cute: *Over Five hundred Satisfied Customers Served…*is a restaurant sign, not one found in the Zodiac!

■ ■ ■

Don't: Overthink it. *OK, you were born again*. Just go with when you get birthday cards.

■ ■ ■

Don't: Say that's horse manure! Suppose they're Chinese and born in the year of the horse? (OK, I'm stretching this one!)

■ ■ ■

Don't: Be boring. Your natal sign is Capricorn and you have two planets in Libra; the only message he'll get is—*too much information*!

■ ■ ■

Absolutely Do Not: Be a celebrity hound. Bragging *you were born at the exact moment as Meryl Streep* only begs the question, *why don't you look as good?*

■ ■ ■

Two Capricorns, two divorces. Coincidence, I think not!
Mel, fifties, divorced twice

■ ■ ■

She did my chart. Said we'd make a great team. We do. What more can I say?
Larry, sixties, divorced

■ ■ ■

The day I find a guy who tells me he's been to an astrologer is the day I find my guy!
GGG, sixty-five, widow

■ ■ ■

My wife got me into reading my horoscope. It would be the first thing we looked at in the papers when we had our morning coffee. It was great fun. We even went to a gypsy fortuneteller when we went to Rome on our last trip before she died. It gave her great hope. Actually, it gave us both peace of mind.
Gavin, seventy-two, widower.

■ ■ ■

My grandmother used to host séances, and I remember she would wrap a gold turban around my head and introduce me to her guests as her personal guide to the spirit world. I was eight, and it was great fun. She got me into reading my horoscope, and I haven't missed a day in what...forty plus years? No, I don't put that in my profile, but when I meet a guy who admits to believing in the spiritual world, you bet, I'll tell him my story.
Gloria, fifty-five, widow

■ ■ ■

My Ideal Match

■ ■ ■

*It is not until you rhyme with a person that makes you their
perfect match,
it is when you are satisfied with each other's peculiarities,
and find jewels in their loopholes.*

—MICHAEL BASSEY JOHNSON

LADIES—THIS IS your chance to go for the brass ring. If you're looking for *Prince Charming* to come along and fit that *Jimmy Chou* on your dainty tootsie…then let's make sure the fella knows your shoe size.

Want a *Christian Grey* from *Fifty Shades of…then let's make* sure he's savvy enough to show up with *mink handcuffs and two, silk scarves.*

Sugar, as in do-re-mi? Well, we have to make sure he knows the difference between dollars and Dominos, don't we?

Hey girl—it's 2016 and, metaphorically speaking, if guys can kick the tires, take it out for a test drive, then shop around until they come up with the perfect ride—so can you little darlin' so can you.

Gentlemen—and now I'm talking to all types—this heading should be titled: *My Ideal Pheromone.* (Do I need to say more?)

(Warning to everyone! Just be careful what you wish for!)

■ ■ ■

Do: Understand the terms. He may think a long-term relationship is four dates. Be ready to negotiate.

■　■　■

Do: Remember you have standards. Think twice before writing *as long as they can put breath on the mirror.*

■　■　■

Don't: Write *Mr./Ms. Right.* Could you be any less original?

■　■　■

Don't: Declare *well-proportioned* when you really mean *hung like a rhino.*

■　■　■

Don't: Brag *like my daddy.* Oh grow up, and stop pretending you're still six!

■　■　■

Don't: Write *a man who knows the meaning of love,* that is, *my house, my rules.*

■　■　■

Don't: Write *something new.* In other words, *you want someone half your age. Cradle robber!*

■　■　■

Don't: Declare you want *an equal* when we know…some of us are more equal than others.

■　■　■

Don't: Say *an affair to remember.* You're thinking *the movie;* he's thinking *you want to film it.*

■　■　■

Don't: Jump the gun. Best to wait and confess that your ultimate fantasy is for your bride to come dressed as a lumberjack.

■　■　■

Don't: Answer every question by adding…*tall, dark and handsome…in bold and capital letters.*

■　■　■

Don't: Forget when you left the divorce proceedings; you swore you'd rather be shot in the head than get involved with another redhead.

■　■　■

Don't: Write *polygamous.* Looking up the definition only increases the odds of him first checking the sports sites; then…*it's sayonara baby.*

■　■　■

Don't: Be old-fashion. You think a date's sharing a straw in a malt shop; he may think sharing bodily fluids in a motel. Be ready with the *pepper spray.*

■　■　■

Don't: Put lipstick on a pig. *Mutually exclusive?* You think he doesn't know that's code for *I'll cut 'em off, if I catch you looking at another woman?*

■　■　■

Don't: Ruin a good thing. He can work around *relationship,* but adding *meaningful* means *rules,* and men hate rules unless they make them.

■　■　■

Absolutely Do Not: Drop the *M Bomb.* When I said *go for the brass ring,* I didn't mean the *wedding ring.* Not saying *substance man* won't marry, but like horses, he needs to be led to water before he drinks; otherwise, he'll run for the hills.

■　■　■

Comfortable, compatible, very loving, and passionate. (What an ideal combination!)
NCB, fifty-nine, divorced

■　■　■

It doesn't take much to make me a happy man, especially when I'm caring for the person in my life.
C, sixty-nine, widower

■　■　■

Honesty. Yes, that is the number one criteria. Then of course it's chemistry. I'm seventy-six, but I'm not dead!
HG, seventy-four, widow

■　■　■

Ideal? Someone who won't cancel on me. It's gotten so bad that many of my women friends are off the Internet. They're not interested in being stood up and rather spend time with their children, grandkids, book clubs, and theater.
CP, fifties, divorced

■ ■ ■

Money, honey. Of course not going to write that, but none of my friends want to give up their quality of life and certainly don't expect to support a guy. Not saying he has to live in a ten million dollar mansion by the water, but it has to be a step up, otherwise it's a step down. I would like to meet someone who is tall, slim, physically fit, respects women, confident, but also knows how to compromise. They can have any hair shade or any eye color.
CP, fifties, divorced

■ ■ ■

Sure, I'm interested in what most other people want…a warm, intelligent, compassionate, fun-loving guy who shares my off-beat sense of humor. I'm happy men find me attractive. In great shape. Smart, energetic, loves to sing, knows the words to most Golden Oldies. I'd also be thrilled to meet someone who shares my love of classical music. I also love to travel, especially to France, Italy, and Africa. Do you like to Ballroom dance? It's one of my favorite ways to keep in shape while having a fabulous time.
Donna, sixty-eight, divorced

■ ■ ■

Their Gender

■ ■ ■

I believe gender is a spectrum,
and I fall somewhere between
Channing Tatum and Winnie the Pooh.

—STEPHEN COLBERT

I HAVE NO idea why a simple male or female response needs to be qualified, exaggerated, or inflated (yep, I'm talking to you ladies).

This is not the place to make veiled innuendos regarding his *package, or cleverly insinuate that anyone who can't get it up need not reply.*

Men—a woman isn't defined by how well she plays *the mouth organ.* (And, don't try to say you were only interested in her musical talents! Last I looked, *flutist wasn't a gender.*)

Finally, this is a question about their gender—not yours! So guys—step away from the mirror and stop looking at your pump-up biceps. And ladies—I wouldn't be strutting around the room singing "Respect," moments before you fill out your answer.

■ ■ ■

Do: Remember you're not a *Goose,* so don't confuse *Gander,* for *gender.*

■ ■ ■

Do: Remember two wrongs don't make a right. So, *SexGodAdam,* don't ask for *SexGodessEve!*

■　■　■

Don't: Write *Big Boy.* Desirable as it may be…not a gender.

■　■　■

Don't: Lose control. *Stripper* is not considered a *gender,* either.

■　■　■

Don't: Let the *Little Head* take control. You are better than that.

■　■　■

Don't: Write *hot-blooded.* Still not an accepted gender outside of Latin America.

■　■　■

Don't: Forget the fundamental nature of your site. *Does an elephant look for a mate in an aviary?*

■　■　■

Don't: Use metaphors. Guys—I already warned you about *mouth organ,* so don't even request someone who plays the *skin flute!*

■　■　■

Don't: Mix up your *Gs*. While excellent attributes: *genial, gentle,* and *genuine* are not *genders.*

■ ■ ■

Don't: Add...*and ready to prove it.* Why put them behind the eight ball when the game hasn't even begun?

■ ■ ■

Don't: Write *Man of Steel* without thinking of the morning after. (That goes for a *Twenty-Four-Hour Man,* too.)

■ ■ ■

Don't: Dream the impossible dream. Come on, who can actually pull a boat across the San Francisco Bay by his teeth?

■ ■ ■

Absolutely Do Not: Add...*Well-endowed.* You can't be satisfied with a little piece of heaven—*you have to have the moon and stars, too?*

■ ■ ■

No more pretending! Thank God for the Internet!
SA, late fifties, single

■ ■ ■

You have to go on a site catering to your gender. Otherwise, at best it's a needle in a haystack, and at the worst, you'll be subject to trolls or thrill seekers.
NCB, fifty-nine, divorced

■　■　■

I've a brother who's straight, and we've both had the same history on the web of meeting lots of great people, but never finding that someone special. Funny thing, at our age, these new friendships seem to overshadow all the negatives.
TKA, fifties, divorced

■　■　■

Their Age Range

■ ■ ■

How was your blind date?
Terrible! He showed up in a 1932 Rolls-Royce.
What's so terrible about that?
He was the original owner.

—Anonymous

Despite the ribbing I get from guys who proudly order from the child's menu for their dinner dates, I have stubbornly held to the view I wanted a woman who remembers the excitement she felt the first time she saw Elvis shake rattle and roll on the *Ed Sullivan Show* or still smiles when she recalls Groucho's witty and unrelenting banter with George Fenneman on *You Bet Your Life*. In other words, someone my own f-ing age!

One online vet thought that commendable, but after she visited a friend at a certain hospital known for knee and hip replacements, she decided she'd take out insurance against that happening to her new mate and began looking for men at least twenty years younger.

When she saw the apprehension in my face, she said, "Don't worry about the sex. If he dies, he dies…"

Well, shut my mouth!

■ ■ ■

Do: Check out your photo album in case you've forgotten how many candles were on your last birthday cake.

■ ■ ■

Do: Man up. *Your breasts should defy the laws of gravity and natural selection?* Come on, *confess you want someone your granddaughter's age.*

■ ■ ■

Do: Woman up! *Young at heart? Just say you don't want a man with stents.*

■ ■ ■

Don't: Write *my contemporary.* Talk about spinning the truth, whatever that is.

■ ■ ■

Don't: Be judgmental. Just write a number, no need to add...*must be ambulatory!*

■ ■ ■

Don't: Reply *old enough to appreciate an older woman,* that is, you want someone just old enough to shave.

■ ■ ■

Don't: Go twenty years higher; in other words; *sugar-sugar, it's summertime-summertime and the living's gonna be easy-easy.*

■ ■ ■

Don't: Go thirty years higher. Code for *one foot in the grave, and I have one unbreakable prenup.*

■ ■ ■

Don't: Be a numbers person and consult an actuary table unless you're prepared to find out when yours is up.

■ ■ ■

Don't: Write *old enough to know better.* Code for *you're a neat freak and will freak out if they leave dirty dishes in the sink.*

■ ■ ■

Absolutely Do Not: Say *if they die, they die* without giving me credit for the joke!

■ ■ ■

65 is the new 56.
GGG, sixty-five, widow

■ ■ ■

I'm out of your age range, but I loved your write-up.
A, seventy-three, widow

■ ■ ■

If you're willing to put up with some age-related back issues, I'm your man.
Jack, fifty-nine, widower

■ ■ ■

It amazes me, men our age still behave like these last forty years haven't existed. I met this one guy at a sports bar, and after the usual get to know you stuff, he points to a woman and says, bet you anything, she likes it bareback.
Gavin, seventy-two, widower

■ ■ ■

If you love someone you have to take the good with the bad. I also know for many of my women friends, this is impossible, and that's why they're not dating. I can't blame them, especially those that recently had to take care of a husband, who after a long illness, passed.
Chris, sixty-seven, divorced

■ ■ ■

I don't want to be anybody's nurse. I know people our age are more likely to get sick, die, and the last thing I want is to be stuck taking care of someone. Hard as it sounds, that's why I like men at least ten years younger. Of course, I'm being selfish. Many men won't want a woman ten years older for the same reason. So far I've been lucky and have someone eleven years my junior for a beau.
Donna, sixty-eight, divorced

■ ■ ■

You've seriously written a laugh-out-loud profile, very clever and amusing. It could have been lifted from a course I taught for many years, "Women and Men: Roles and Relationships in Contemporary Society." Bravo! And if your answer is "yes" to chatting with a woman around your age and single—meaning you don't subscribe to old-fashioned notions of how a woman must be younger and married at least once—I'd like that.
Linda, sixty, widow

■ ■ ■

One of the hottest women I met was over eighty. I'm seventy-two, and wasn't looking for anyone over seventy-five, but I have to say I was very tempted. She had work done and looked fifty. She also had her breasts enlarged and always wore low-cut outfits that really turned me on. What turned me off was when she took me to her house and removed her jacket, and I could see how unappealing her upper arms were. I know, I shouldn't be so picky, but I just had to get out of there.

Gavin, seventy-two, widower

■　■　■

Believe me, everything they say about young guys wanting to learn new tricks from women our age is absolutely true! I can't tell you how many guys in their twenties write me—actually tell me I'm the perfect person to teach them all about sex. I'm sixty-five. I was married for forty-eight years, and Hal was the only guy I've ever slept with. Of course, I don't actually say that in my profile, about Hal that is, but I don't know what books, movies these guys are reading that make them believe I'm an expert in lovemaking? Look, I just got another one. Nineteen and thinks I look like Faye Dunaway. Well, that's a new one. Usually it's Sharon Stone.

GGG, sixty-five, widow

■　■　■

The hardest thing is you have to get over their jealousy. Soon as you tell friends you're dating a guy twenty years younger, they give you a look like you're crazy. Then they give you all the standard excuses. He wants older women, because they're desperate, horny, and it's a quick screw. Or, he wants a Sugar Mama. Or, he's looking for his mother and wants to breastfeed. That's not funny, but what is funny/ironic is, when I introduced them to Jeff, they all went gaga. You should see them flirting with him and, to top it all off, now they're all asking me, to ask him, to fix them up. Can you imagine? Of course, they're some who are still jealous. Mostly the girls at Mahjong.

I'm thinking of giving my weekly game up, anyway. Jeff wants to take up mountain climbing.
FC, fifty-nine, divorced

■ ■ ■

Their Marital Status

■ ■ ■

Half the lies they tell about me aren't true.

—Yogi Berra

This section should be named: *Calling Miss Marple.* Time after time, women have told me they were becoming amateur detectives and were employing various websites to check up on the marital status of the men they intended to meet, because they were sick and tired of being lied to, only to discover, when it was too late, he was married or otherwise involved.

One woman quipped: "I felt like calling the pet detective, *Ace Ventura,* because I didn't want to meet another dog like Drew." (You better believe I changed his name and cleaned that one up!).

Men I spoke with told me they never went to such lengths. They were totally surprised when I informed of what the women said. I received a chorus of: "Not by me, or I'd never lie about my marital status!"

I was divorced by the time I went online, so I'm not going to stand in judgment on anyone who does deceive, except to warn those who are thinking about it...what chance do you have with *Ace Ventura* on your case?

■ ■ ■

Do: Understand *Momma's Boy* is not a legitimate category, whether you want one or not.

■ ■ ■

Do: Think positive and remember *waterboarding* is always an option if you *suspect they're been lying.*

■ ■ ■

Don't: Choose *Activity Partner* unless you're into *orgies.*

■ ■ ■

Don't: Declare *divorced* because your wife's using her maiden name.

■ ■ ■

Don't: Write *jilted* because you want someone to commiserate with.

■ ■ ■

Don't: Add…*divorced twice* because you believe three times a charm.

■ ■ ■

Don't: Say *no experience necessary.* There you go again, *robbing the cradle.*

■ ■ ■

Don't: Proclaim *all of the above* in block letters. Show some dignity, will you!

■ ■ ■

Don't: Add…*desperately seeking a…*That just makes you sound–well—*desperate!*

■ ■ ■

Don't: Think the worse. Not all *widowers* kill their wives; so, don't ask if there was an inquest.

■　■　■

Don't: Declare *separated* when you sleep in another room, because they hate your snoring.

■　■　■

Don't: Go off-topic. *Virile* is not a marital status, no matter what you read in *Elle or Girls' Life*.

■　■　■

Don't: Editorialize. Sure, you had a bad marriage, but it's a little harsh to write *divorced guys are lowlifes*.

■　■　■

Don't: Say you're looking for someone who's been *widowed and then add…* because *misery loves company*.

■　■　■

Absolutely Do Not: Write *I don't care as long as you'll love me.* The first thing he'll think is—*there you go*—*putting strings on the relationship, and we haven't even met.*

■　■　■

E-mail once, maybe twice, and just one call. If you can't tolerate the voice, they're done. Do men lie? Yep, yep, and yep! Weight, height, finances, but

specially about their marital status. If they won't give you their home phone or take you by their house...you bet your life they've got a wife.
Linda, sixties, widow

■　■　■

It used to be you looked for the ring. Then it was the white band where the ring used to be. Now I just expect if they're too good to be true somebody else got 'em first. So why am I still looking? I'm an optimist.
CD, fifties, divorced

■　■　■

Look, I'm a trusting person. That's who I am. So when a guy says he's single, or divorced, I believe him. I can't go through life being suspicious like some of my friends. No, I don't go onto the web to check guys out. No, I don't ask men for their home phones, or call men late at night on their cells. Honestly, I haven't had a lot of dates, and certainly none turned into long-term relationships. And, as far as I know, the men have been truthful. Am I 100 percent sure? Who knows? One thing I am sure of, in spite of all the horror stories I hear from my girlfriends, I am not going to change.
Laura, late sixties, widow

■　■　■

We met online. I think she contacted me. We had dinner at a college club, and she treated. This was a first. When we met she said, "Welcome to where I usually have dinner." She had been married four times and apparently the last marriage was the best. Tragically, he had died suddenly. We had a very nice dinner and discovered we had been born in the same town and still vacationed there in the summer. Seemed like a perfect Internet connection. Two days later, I received an e-mail that said, while she had had a lovely time, being with me reminded her of her deceased husband. She asked to be a friend and to keep in contact. I thought it over, decided, why not. I e-mailed her and said I would

like that. I continued trying to contact her for about a week, but there was no response.
Steve, midsixties, widower

■　■　■

After a year of living dangerously, I decided I would only date widowers but not just any widower, but ones that had been married for more than ten years, had children, and most important, hadn't lost their wives within the last six months. My girlfriend Merrill told me horror stories about men recently widowed; how all they did was talk about their dead wives until you wanted to jump into their graves just to get these guys to stop crying in their soup. I don't need to tell you this limited my choices, but there were a few. Jason is the one I remember most. We met for cocktails. It took about half an hour before the subject of his late wife came up. We were talking about food, how I love to make soups that last me for the week. His eyes lit up. That's when he told me his dying wife made sure he had a freezer full upon her demise and that's what he was eating. I was stunned, reminded him in his profile he wrote she had died a year ago. That's right…a year ago…and he was still enjoying the home cooking.
Linda, sixties, widow

■　■　■

Their Religion

■ ■ ■

The only thing that counts is faith
expressing itself through love.

—Galatians 5:6

Remember why you're on the site. Consider your own persuasion or lack of any specific belief system. Most of all, understand selecting a site simply because it seems a cultural fit can have its drawbacks. OK, you like a bagel with a smear, but that's a little superficial, don't you think? What about joining a Catholic dating site because you want to commiserate with others who had a nun rap them on the knuckles in the second grade?

(Warning! If all newcomers are invited to a picnic in your area, hightail it out of there if, upon arrival, everyone is naked and chanting for you to come forward and dance around a boiling cauldron.)

■ ■ ■

Do: Understand, *Eros is not an organized religion.*

■ ■ ■

Don't: Ask for the moon. Not all *Catholic know the pope personally.*

■ ■ ■

Don't: Add…*but not practicing.* Makes you look like you *can't commit.*

■　■　■

Don't: Declare you are *a true believer,* that is, *you'll fall for any line they feed you.*

■　■　■

Don't: Be picky. When you get down to it, what's the real difference between *pagan* and *culturally pagan?*

■　■　■

Don't: Be really, really picky. *A follower of Zoroastrianism but only on their mother's side*—come on—really?

■　■　■

Don't: Declare *you are hoping for a practicing atheist* but will take *agnostic.* Nobody wants someone who just settles.

■　■　■

Don't: Write *the Sun God.* Same as *nature worshiper,* clever, nevertheless; codes for *you better look damn fine in a Speedo.*

■　■　■

Don't: Be looking for miracles. If want him to turn wine into water, stick to sites aimed at guys who own vineyards, not ones that rely on Bible stories.

■　■　■

Absolutely Do Not: Think *reformed* means they no longer cheat on their mate.

■   ■   ■

"Will tell you later" only means trouble if you're on a religious site.
Linda, sixties, widow

■   ■   ■

My daughter has no problem with dating guys not of her faith, but I find that every Irish Protestant women over sixty-five that I'm attracted to seems to have a hard time with an Italian Roman Catholic gentlemen like myself.
Gavin, seventy-two, widower

■   ■   ■

I run deep. Life can be fun, but some things have to be taken seriously. Commitment to friends and family means a lot to me. I enjoy doing fun things, but am always there to help with life's curveballs. Am more spiritual than religious, but am open to all faiths.
LC, fifties, single

■   ■   ■

What are important are family, faith, honesty, and respect. Then I believe a sense of humor is necessary if we're to successfully deal with the hardships in life. I also have a desire to let loose sometimes and hope he would be able to show the same kind of spontaneity. Music is magical, and I like to listen to many genres, and dancing can be so romantic. Will send phone number upon request.
Donna, sixty-eight, divorced

■   ■   ■

He was Italian and I'm Jewish, and we had been dating for a month without our religions being a factor. It didn't become a problem until the evening he first introduced me to his friends as: "Kathy, she's Jewish." When I mentioned it, he brushed it off, said he didn't mean anything by it. Unfortunately, he did it again when he brought me to meet his sister. I kept my cool. It was only when he took me home I told him I was offended and I was ending our relationship. He called, messaged me, even sent me flowers, but I never responded.
Gloria, fifty-five, widow

■   ■   ■

Their Education

■ ■ ■

Not that we were incompatible;
we just had nothing to talk about.

—Haruki Murakami

I'M NO EDUCATION snob. Just because he has a *monosyllabic vocabulary* and she does the *Friday New York Times crossword puzzle in ink* doesn't mean they can't have a meaningful relationship.

Liar, liar, pants on fire!

OK, OK, you got me. A beautiful face is alluring, but can only hold my attention as long as she can hold an engaging conversation.

No question, a terrific body is a turn-on, but nothing turns me off faster than when her subjects don't agree with her verbs.

All I'm saying…if you crave meaningful conversations on global warming, I'd be looking for someone who majored in *earth science*, not a business grad who thinks *bean counters* should run the world.

Think commonality. Think…Ken and Barbie. Think…Dos and Don'ts.

■ ■ ■

Do: Remember the *School of Hard Knocks is not accredited.*

■ ■ ■

Don't: Be unrealistic. How many boomers know their SAT scores?

■ ■ ■

Don't: Require him to speak Japanese because you'll get better sushi.

■ ■ ■

Don't: Wish for a *Phi Beta Kappa* unless you're ready to fondle their key.

■ ■ ■

Don't: Be absurd. What does knowing their average Scrabble score have to do with this question?

■ ■ ■

Don't: Declare *legacies need not apply.* Just because their fathers endowed the college library doesn't mean they're all dumb as a stump.

■ ■ ■

Don't: Be a pig. *Cheerleading? Drum Majorette?* Besides not being a course of study, they were out of your league then, and even more so, now.

■ ■ ■

Don't: Say *homeschooling*, that is, nothing in common with someone who loves cafeteria food and can't resist carving his or her name on wooden desks.

■ ■ ■

Don't: Be a *nit*. If you want someone with a British private school education, don't say *Red Brick:* just ask if they *attended Oxford or Cambridge.*

■   ■   ■

Don't: Add restrictions. Isn't it enough they can complete Friday's *Times* Crossword? Does it have to be in ink? (I'm repeating myself, but I hear this all the time.)

■   ■   ■

Don't: Ask *"Et qui es-tu au juste?"* You majored in French lit, but that doesn't mean you have to be a show-off. (They may know the saying and ask: *"And just who might you be?" The worm turns, does it not?*)

■   ■   ■

Absolutely Do Not: Write *some*. You want them to read or not?

■   ■   ■

I've had guys tell me they went to Harvard and later found out attended BU or Emerson. Don't they know you can look up college yearbooks on the web?
CP, fifties, divorced

■   ■   ■

Seeing all those degrees can be a little intimidating, especially for someone like me who only has a BA, but it comes down to how nice the gentleman is. That's true is any relationship.
Karen P, late fifties, divorced

■   ■   ■

Look, I'm in my seventies and not interested in reliving my college years, but I find I have more in common with women who've had those experiences, and I feel more comfortable with someone who's had at least a year or two of college. Terry, seventies, divorced

■ ■ ■

I find there is a correlation between education and an ability to be informed. A man with a background in the social sciences is the kind of guy I'm attracted to. Laura, late sixties, widow

■ ■ ■

Do They Smoke/Nonsmoker

■ ■ ■

I've never dated a smoker
but if Don Draper looked my way,
I'd drop my panties in a second.
Seriously though, I don't think I could deal with the smell.
Yuck.

—MELISSA NIBBLES

MY FRIEND, FRITZ, is a fool for cigars, but more a fool for any woman smoking them. Imagine what happens when he spots a photo of an alluring woman seductively puffing on a cigar, usually in a sexy outfit, and always in an exotic seaside locale?

Unfortunately, every woman he's met fitting this profile also has a desire for mescal. (So the worm turns. His words, not mine.)

He's hoping a concoction of Pepto and almond soy milk that he swallows beforehand will coat his stomach, and do the trick, because he's just off to San Diego to meet Lola who can't have her *Cohiba Exquisito* without her *gusano*.

■ ■ ■

Do: Remember this is a dating site, so just answer the question and leave out the images of skull and crossbones.

■ ■ ■

Don't: Make them feel anymore threatened by referring to cigarettes as *coffin sticks.*

■   ■   ■

Don't: Say never smoked, then take a picture showing your *Nicorette patch, and tell them it's a Band-Aid from your flu shot.*

■   ■   ■

Don't: Say *for medicinal purposes or recreational use only,* as they are code for *I'm ready to move to Colorado—you?*

■   ■   ■

Don't: Put conditions to his smoking like: *Sure, if you want to give yourself and anyone within a hundred feet of you lung cancer.*

■   ■   ■

Don't: Brag. Maybe at twenty, you could share a drag or two, but now the only thing you'll be sucking is *wind after a tussle in the sheets.*

■   ■   ■

Don't: Declare *only after a brandy.* First it's *Grand Marnier,* then a *Pouilly-Fuissé,* and then *Michelob.* You tell me, where will it end…*Dr. Pepper?*

■   ■   ■

Don't: Make exceptions. *Pipes?* Only if he wears a *deerstalkers cap, lives at 221B Baker Street, and answers to the name, Sherlock.*

■   ■   ■

Don't: Be stupid. OK, you think you look like James Dean in the photo, but you've got a cigarette dangling from your mouth and you wrote *nonsmoker!*

■ ■ ■

Absolutely Do Not: Be a hypocrite. If you wrote *Gauloises* because it makes you feel like Brigitte Bardot, why can't he smoke *Monopoli di stato* if it makes him feel like Clint Eastwood in *The Good, the Bad and the Ugly?*

■ ■ ■

Idiot said he didn't smoke, but when I looked him up on Facebook, saw him lying on a deck chair with a huge cigar in his mouth.
FC, fifty-nine, divorced

■ ■ ■

Big problem. Great photo. Even better in person, but smelled the smoke on her clothes the minute we hugged. Didn't want to hurt her feelings, so I made up some story about how it was just too soon after my wife's death for me to date.
Jack, fifty-nine, widower

■ ■ ■

I wouldn't say this is the biggest lie. Hair and weight still rank higher. Numbers? One of five, and you won't find out until the third date when they think you're so taken with them they pull out their fancy Cubans and brag how they cleverly smuggle them into the country.
Ellyn, late fifties, divorced

■ ■ ■

Nice, well-spoken gentlemen. We met for a stroll in the park. He offered me a stick of gum. Said he just gave up cigarettes. I did the same, but I chew too loudly, so I didn't want to turn him off and I declined. After a few minutes, he says gum's lost its flavor and spits it out in the direction of a trashcan. Whizzed right by my face. Turned my stomach. No idea how I made it through the park. CW, fifties, widow

■   ■   ■

Their Drinking Habits

■ ■ ■

In wine there is wisdom,
in beer there is Freedom,
in water there is bacteria.

—BENJAMIN FRANKLIN

REMEMBER, HOW I handled this question? I had to stop with the giggles and the vino. What I'm saying is—don't throw stones—but also be realistic.

I certainly didn't want a teetotaler or my dinner date waving a temperance banner; something on the lines of: *I'm on the Water Wagon, and I'm Better off.*

On the other hand, I didn't want a five-martini-lunch-lady, or a woman who only dined where a sommelier could provide her with *the correct white burgundy to go with her Salad Nicoise.*

So—follow my Dos and Don'ts and fill out this profile responsibly.

■ ■ ■

Do: Heed previous warnings, and don't answer unless you can touch your nose with the tip of your finger while reciting *Peter Piper picked a peck of pickled peppers five times...without giggling.*

■ ■ ■

Don't: Say *socially,* that is, *you're a friendly drunk.*

■ ■ ■

Don't: Be judgmental. *No falling-down drunkards need apply...* Really?

■ ■ ■

Don't: Write *not at all* because there'll be times you'll want to see them *dance on a table.*

■ ■ ■

Don't: Make it into a competition. Not everyone finds it fun to *drink shots until one of you falls off the barroom stool.*

■ ■ ■

Don't: Be a wine snob. Come on, you actually think if they ordered a *78'* instead of a *79' Montrachet,* you'd know the difference?

■ ■ ■

Don't: Limit them to *occasionally* as that can be confused with: *When the occasion strikes—like every afternoon at Four.*

■ ■ ■

Don't: Generalize. OK, you don't trust a person who doesn't drink but to call teetotalers *lower than the fungus that feeds on pond scum...?*

■ ■ ■

Don't: Harp on your screen name. Obviously, *FiveMartiniLunch* is ample proof *(no pun intended)* you'd like someone who likes a cocktail or two at noon.

■　■　■

Absolutely Do Not: Add…*in moderation.* That's almost as bad as asking them to drink responsibly.

■　■　■

I'm sure someone has told you about how they invite you for a coffee date and end up ordering two or more glasses of wine. I try to be as kind as I can and make up some story as to why I have to leave.
Donna, sixty-eight, divorced

■　■　■

Nobody is going to admit they have a problem. My advice? Like everything else in a new relationship, take it slow. If he's having two cocktails and a bottle of wine for dinner and then wants to drive home, I'd take a cab.
Nan, fifty-nine, divorced

■　■　■

I had the unfortunate experience of falling for what I thought was a nice, old-fashioned girl until I met up with her and her girlfriend at a local bar and watched them down tequila shooters until they drank two members of a local biker gang under the table.
Steve, midsixties, widower

■　■　■

You've been looking in the wrong places. We are all not party animals, looking for a one-night stand or a "Goodtime Charlie." There are women who are sober, centered, happy with whom they are, have created wonderful lives for themselves, and just want to share some of that joy. Are you up to that kind of challenge?
KK, late fifties, widow

■   ■   ■

At our age it is unrealistic to think a majority of us don't have one addiction or another. I'm having a terrible time giving up sugar and just last year gave up smoking (for the umpteenth time). Hope this one lasts. For me, it's a matter of what I can put up with. No smokers, nobody that busts me about my weight, and nobody who can't hold their liquor or becomes abusive when they drink.
Cal, fifties, divorced twice

■   ■   ■

Their Dietary Restrictions

■ ■ ■

Focus on eating real, whole, natural foods.
As I love to say,
if you can pick it, pluck it,
milk it, or shoot it,
you can eat it!

—SUZANNE SOMERS

WHEN I CONFESSED to an online vet who also happens to be a transplanted Carolinian that I required libation to get through the *drinking sections*, she grinned, admitted in her case, it wasn't vino, but filling her face with mashed potatoes and grits.

As luck would have it, a Southern-style deli whose specialty is this very dish, recently opened up just around the corner, and instead of going through the time and energy to make her own, she orders in and logs in with unbridled confidence.

When I asked if she placed any restrictions on a prospect, she admitted she preferred men from the South, although adding grits to the mash wasn't an absolute must.

You don't have to love soul food to search your own soul, but remember when dealing with dietary restrictions, you're actually making sure you won't be deprived of your foodie obsessions. Keep in mind how unpleasant you become if you can't have that crispy slice of bacon on your Eggos!

■ ■ ■

Do: Make it clear that *dining out* doesn't mean going to a *drive-through*.

■　■　■

Do: Declare *no picky eaters* if you love *all-you-can-eat buffet deals*.

■　■　■

Do: Find out if they hate *Moonshine* because you need to see *Kinfolk on the holidays*.

■　■　■

Do: Stick to your guns. If they're serving *Coq au vin*, they must use *French cookware*.

■　■　■

Don't: Tie diet to clothing. Some men just love to eat pizza in their *skivvies*.

■　■　■

Don't: Limit their *liquid lunches* to *a power smoothie* unless you're ready to run a mile in their shoes.

■　■　■

Don't: Confuse them. When you're a vegan and write down dishes like *Mongolian stir-fry BBQ*, you're sending mixed messages.

■　■　■

Don't: Beat around the bush and ask if he has a food allergy when you really want to know if he's allergic to spending money at five-star restaurants.

■　■　■

Absolutely Do Not: Declare *the only grill they'll ever see is the one on my car when I run the sucker over.*

■　■　■

I can't stop eating bread and would like a man who hates the stuff. Nah, even for love, I couldn't give up my dinner rolls.
Helen, fifties, divorced

■　■　■

Now I am looking for a man who is thirsty to drink from the fountain of magical experiences, no kosher laws required.
LKS, sixties, single

■　■　■

In the beginning, I didn't have any friends giving me advice, so I didn't see anything wrong with going to dinner with a man I'd never met. We have a cocktail, nice conversation, then dinner.
Do you know what a gastric bypass is? When the patient has to wear a gastric belly belt?
Yes, I've heard of them.
Do you know anything about their eating habits? I'll tell you, they eat slowly, very slowly. Because I'm a doctor, I diagnosed the problem, but I didn't want to be intrusive or insensitive, but after an agonizing half-hour of watching him take one tiny bite after another, I finally asked if he had the surgery.
And?
At first, he didn't want to admit it, but when I told him I was a doctor...

You hadn't mentioned it in your profile?
No, I just wrote medical professional. He finally confessed and hoped it wouldn't make a difference. I told him I didn't think we were a match and excused myself and left. I'm sorry, it probably doesn't sound nice, but I couldn't imagine watching him eat for another hour, much less another minute.
LLK, sixties, divorced

■　■　■

Their Income Level

■ ■ ■

While money can't buy happiness,
it certainly lets you choose
your own form of misery.

—GROUCHO MARX

IF YOU FOLLOWED my advice to be cautious and circumspect and left your income level blank or wrote *will tell you later* until you got to know the individual better and felt you could trust them with this important information, it would be to your advantage to leave this question blank as well. Otherwise, you could be accused of being disingenuous at best and a money-grubbing so-and-so at worst.

Friends who live in Florida confess the money issue comes up when prospects from up north want to visit but don't want to stay in a hotel. Sure, sex is on their minds, but these friends tell me it's a sure sign the prospect either doesn't have the money, or is too cheap to spend it, both very strong indications the relationship is doomed.

Another veteran used to play *I tell you mine, if you tell me yours* but discovered her dates played another game of *walking it back* when they met for a coffee date.

Remember what another vet said: *There's no romance without finance.* I might add, *there's none without a little humor, either.*

■ ■ ■

Do: Ask if he knows what a *vig is* to find out if he owes a loan shark.

■ ■ ■

Do: Ask if he has a lawyer on speed dial to discover if he has any *civil suits pending.*

■ ■ ■

Do: Ask for the expiration date on his *black card,* by far the *cleverest way to find a sugar daddy.*

■ ■ ■

Do: Ask for a *Sunny Day Number* then a *Rainy Day one,* divide by two, and see if *your sun's going to shine tomorrow.*

■ ■ ■

Don't: Do movie quotes and ask, *"If his ego is writing checks his body can't cash."*

■ ■ ■

Don't: Add…*nothing wrong with leaving one man for another, as long as the second guy has more money.*

■ ■ ■

Don't: Ask if the bed's adjustable, that is, you want to know *how much money's stashed under the mattress.*

■ ■ ■

Don't: Ask if they *rent or own*. That may have meant something before the mortgage crisis, but not anymore.

■ ■ ■

Don't: Let your love of Ballroom Dancing cloud your eyes and confess you don't care if they don't have a pot to pee in, as long as you love to Tango.

■ ■ ■

Don't: Use euphemisms. *Earn a comfortable living?* Damn it! Just come right out and say *you're high maintenance.*

■ ■ ■

Absolutely Do Not: Add...*and after you send me your returns, I'll be showing them to my forensic accountant.*

■ ■ ■

I check everyone out. Saves a lot of heartache this way.
CP, fifties, divorced

■ ■ ■

The fancier the car, the bigger the house, the more debts. Believe me. I know.
Ellyn, late fifties, divorced

■ ■ ■

I thought writing about my lifestyle would be enough to lead men to understand they needed a certain income if they were to share my life. I was wrong.
Gloria, fifty-five, widow

■   ■   ■

It's easy to be a target if you're not comfortable with yourself. I made a good living and didn't need to depend on a man or a marriage to be comfortable. That's not to say I want to support a man. I don't. The best of all worlds would be for each of us to be equal partners.
Chris, sixty-seven, divorced

■   ■   ■

The Short Answer Questionnaire

■ ■ ■

Shall I compare thee to a summer's day?

—WILLIAM SHAKESPEARE, *SONNET 18*

RECENTLY, DATING SITES have taken a giant step forward to the benefit of all *dating kind.* They have gone beyond the simple *yes/no/check here/format* to provide an exciting new opportunity for you to expand on your essay.

This is wonderful news. However, you must always remember the more effusive you become, the more chance to inadvertently wave a red flag, prompting the reader to have another reason to wave you off. This issue is compounded by the fact many of these sections have seemingly innocent-sounding names that can lure you into a dangerous state of complacency.

Now that I've alerted you to these tender traps, let's immediately use this opportunity and brush away the tiniest chance of a misunderstanding, false impression, or misapprehension that may have occurred during the previous sections.

Sure, you have two grown children, but your new paramour won't have to share the bathroom or be afraid to wear their unmentionables at breakfast, because you will make it absolutely clear...*the kids don't live at home—end of story!*

Sure, your two wives died unexpectedly, but you have the medical examiner's report stating there wasn't enough evidence to warrant an inquest and you've been assured...no DNA evidence can be obtained once the body's been cremated—end of story!

Men—once you've reassured them that their first impressions were irrefutably accurate, now you must seize upon the opportunity to make short work of these short-answer sections with succinct but clever and brilliant responses that continue to dazzle, charm, and reinforce their desire for you.

Ladies—you're glam, beguiling, and your irresistible allure has caught the eye of *Substance Man*. Now it's time to open them even wider and make certain he never loses sight of the fact that you are—*perfectly perfect*.

■　■　■

I'm a retired attorney, and I look at every answer carefully.
Mel, fifties, divorced twice

■　■　■

Yes, yes, and yes! Are we in sync or not! Waiting for your response.
AY, seventies, divorced

■　■　■

The past is past. The future is before us. Is that brief enough for you?
Jack, fifty-nine, widower

■　■　■

Most of the women I've contacted haven't even filled out these sections.
Hank, sixty, widower

■　■　■

I'm not so good at writing long essays or reading them, so I prefer this section.
Nan, fifty-nine, divorced

■　■　■

Aside from a few unpredictable nuances, I think I love you! Awaiting your reply.
RS, forties, single

■　■　■

From what guys tell me, it's my picture. After that, I could just close eyes and answer the question for all it matters.
Laura, late sixties, widow

■　■　■

I am writing to you because your replies appear shallow, self-serving, and Neanderthal. Are you so out-of-touch with what a modern woman wants, or as your seventies' years indicate, still living in a time when women were only good for having babies, cooking dinner, and keeping their mouths shut?
(Let's say, I'm leaving name out to avoid undue retribution, The Author)

■　■　■

The problem…I fell in love without ever meeting him. I know, everybody tells me now; don't take what they say in their profile so seriously. I couldn't help it. We both loved PBS, especially "Frontline." Unfortunately, when we met in person, there was no chemistry. C'est la vie!
Linda, sixties, widow

■　■　■

Talk about luck. We connect, fall in love, and marry. What's amazing is we're on a site that asks a lot of questions. At the end they ask "what you must have" and "what you absolutely can't stand." For some reason, neither of us gets that far. I have cats, am afraid of motorcycles. He's allergic to the furry

creatures, rides a Harley. If we had gotten to those questions, we would never have met!
Chris, sixty-seven, divorced

■   ■   ■

My Life and Ambition

■ ■ ■

My personal ambition remains the same—
to be creative, to be modern,
to stay one step ahead,
to enjoy life.

—NATALIE MASSENET

THE NIGHT BEFORE I filled out my profile I had another *Al Bundy Dream*. I'm a shoe salesman in a high-end department store. I'm ogling swarms of rich and beautiful women and can't wait to fondle their feet when they suddenly begin yelling and screaming; demanding I get them this pair of *Manolos* or that pair of *Jimmy Choos*. I become so overwhelmed, so distraught, I leap up, run to an open window and jump twenty-floors to my death.

Wow, let me say, I suddenly feel so much better now that I've told somebody!

I bet you that has happened to you! I'll wager right now, you have a desire, dream, or secret you're dying to disclose, and what better place to unburden your soul than on a dating site!
No! No! No!

Aside from the obvious that I should stop binge-watching *Married with Children*, revealing my dream could be interpreted to mean I can't take orders from women, I have a foot fetish or something construed to be far more disturbing—I'm disturbed.

What I am trying to tell you in the gentlest of ways is...this is not the place to confess that ever since you smashed open your first watermelon, you wanted to be a brain surgeon only, somebody had to work the farm or...you wanted to be the first woman to be an NFL linebacker, but you had to follow in your mom's footsteps and sell jewelry on QVC.

To paraphrase Jack Webb's famous line on "Dragnet," just the facts, baby boomers, just the facts.

■ ■ ■

Do: Remember your fear of heights when you say *I've always wanted to go cliff–diving into a dime-size pool of sparkling water.*

■ ■ ■

Do: Understand this isn't a sentencing hearing and promise *to learn from my mistakes and become a productive member of society.*

■ ■ ■

Do: Remember you're not a *Miss America Contestant,* so no references to *feeding the hungry, healing the sick, and bringing peace to mankind.*

■ ■ ■

Don't: Send mixed messages and declare you are one of those people who *get high on life.*

■ ■ ■

Don't: Say your great wish is to be *forgiven,* that is, *you've killed someone and are terminally tormented by guilt.*

■ ■ ■

Don't: Say *I will continue to follow my dreams wherever they take me*, that is, *you're the oldest boomer who still sleepwalks.*

■ ■ ■

Don't: Bring up childhood fantasy of *walking in space,* because *baby boomers find it hard enough to ambulate on earth.*

■ ■ ■

Don't: Begin with *please forgive me, I'm new to the dating scene,* that is, code for *it's my party, and I'll look for sympathy if I want to.*

■ ■ ■

Don't: Live in the past and confess there's nothing more special than *climbing on Daddy's knee and telling him what you did that day.*

■ ■ ■■ ■ ■

Don't: Refer to *dreams, nightmares, hallucinations, messages from space,* or any other ways you have been informed by your subconscious.

■ ■ ■

Don't: Confess if you don't hit a *hundred tennis balls off the bedroom wall* before you go to sleep, you'll have no chance to win the *club championship.*

■ ■ ■

Don't: Rant. I know we all hate cable, but this isn't the place to bitch and moan about how they keep raising their prices without improving the service.

■ ■ ■

Absolutely Do Not: Generate any *automatic replies* such as: *X hasn't answered this question yet; Want to ask a question and see their answer? Send an e-mail to start up a conversation.* (Sorry, should have warned you as they're code for: I'm such a pathetic loser with nothing to say that I need this website to come up with an answer.)

■　■　■

Handholding with someone who won't let me slip. I know—hokey, but true.
Helen, fifties, divorced

■　■　■

To enjoy my life to the fullest from here on and to be with someone who appreciates me so I can give back the love we both deserve.
Jack, fifty-nine, widower

■　■　■

I love to cook. I enjoy going into the city but always love coming home to the beach. I love the arts and love to travel. I am honest, sweet and fun to be with. My hope is to find someone who shares these values and values me as much as I value them.
RS, forties, single

■　■　■

Many women I know are desperate. Can't be by themselves. They think their life is incomplete without a man. I find that insulting. You don't need a man to make you happy. My life's ambition? To have a complete and fulfilling life, and if it means sharing that with a man, fine. If not, just as fine.
CP, fifties, divorced

■　■　■

You look like the kind of guy who will spontaneously drive up to see the turning of the leaves, or join me and the rest of the Polar Bear Club in jumping into the freezing December waters off Coney Island. This is just small part of who I am but a "big" part of what our future will be like! Are you up for it?
UR, sixties, divorced twice

■ ■ ■

Romantic, passionate about…listening to music, seeing the sun in the morning, finds out what's going on in the news! And Coffee! That's what I look forward to. What you see in me and what you get is a best friend, confidant. Plus, I give 100 percent of me as your complimentary other half! Perky blonde (yes we do have more fun!), with big blue eyes and a huge, romantic heart. I don't think I'm asking for too much, do you?
KJK, fifties, single

■ ■ ■

A Brief History of My Life

■ ■ ■

I yam, what I yam.

—Popeye

WHAT A QUESTION? Where to start? Where to end? I certainly understood the need for brevity in my essay, but what about here?

I called a friend for advice, but instead of cautioning me against writing my version of *David Copperfield,* she warned me to make sure I didn't fib.

Fib! How dare she think I'd do that? Before I could finish my scolding she cleared the air. Your family—they're checking out your family on Ancestary.com!

I couldn't believe it until she explained that in the good old days, when you met a date face-to-face, you usually went to their home, met the parents, understood *if you saw Mom hit Dad with the newspaper backside the head, your date probably would do the same if you ever left a dirty coffee cup in the sink.*

In addition, there were family photos scattered around your date's house so you could see with your own eyes, if any in her gene pool smiled manically into the camera as they proudly held a bloody axe up for all to see. It was these little clues that usually tipped you off to the fact it was time to beat feet.

What about photos posted on profiles? Don't they serve the same purpose?

My friend snorted with laughter; told me of her girlfriend who got snookered by a guy who had never been married but created a virtual family on a camping site to fool her into thinking he had been.

It might have been then, that the idea of writing this book came into my head.

■　■　■

Do: Remember you're writing for a dating site, not a movie so...no terms like *Fade In, Cut To,* or *Flashback To,* unless you're a member of *The Screenwriters Guild.*

■　■　■

Don't: Confess *high maintenance* doesn't even begin to describe your needs.

■　■　■

Don't: Begin with *after my husband shot himself.* In other words, *life begins after death?*

■　■　■

Don't: Think choosing a tiny font allows you to write your own version of *War and Peace.*

■　■　■

Don't: Live in the past. It seems like yesterday you won *Olympic Gold in the pole vault? Really?*

■　■　■

Don't: Declare *I was married to the prefect man,* that is, *I'll be watching to see if you use the correct salad fork.*

■　■　■

Don't: Start with *I've been the founder and CEO of a Fortune 500 Company...* unless you're looking for *investors*.

■   ■   ■

Don't: Leave out the *murder trial,* but acknowledge you've learned from your mistakes and is a better person for it.

■   ■   ■

Don't: Write *you grew up on the wrong side of the tracks* when it was a subway line that ran under Lexington Avenue.

■   ■   ■

Don't: Confess you *married your nursery school sweetheart.* That only proves you fell for the first child to offer you a sweet.

■   ■   ■

Don't: Confuse *My Life* to mean *My Lives* and write *you were Cleopatra and have the bite of an asp on your derrière to prove it.*

■   ■   ■

Don't: Think you're the second coming of Charles Dickens. Do I have to say it again? Do not begin with, *"It was the best of times, it was the worst of times..."*

■   ■   ■

Don't: Brag as a *single mom; you put two kids through college and now they're lawyers.* Might as well add...*and ready to sue you, if you screw with me.*

■   ■   ■

Absolutely Do Not: Cite *Hannibal Lecter…*say…*over time you'll learn more than you ever want to know…*Nobody wants to be served up with fava beans and a nice Chianti for dinner.

■ ■ ■

Have boat, will travel.
Mel, fifties, divorced twice

■ ■ ■

There is nothing brief about it.
Harry, eighties, widower

■ ■ ■

So much to tell, so little space.
Beth, fifties, single

■ ■ ■

What can I do for you? My list of credits is too long to fit into the message box.
JJ, seventies, widow

■ ■ ■

Fully recovered from a serious illness and simply want to enjoy the rest of my life with a woman who appreciates and loves life as much as I do.
Val, seventies, widower

■ ■ ■

Bit of a back problem from sneaking into too many second movies…Just to let you know, full-time writer who can't afford to travel until Oprah plugs my book.
Jackie, sixties, single

■   ■   ■

I'm a widow who has been blessed with a happy and fulfilling thirty-five-year marriage. Raised two children who are successful, married and happy. Looking for my next chapter to be equally full of love and happiness.
Connie, sixty-eight, widow

■   ■   ■

I am an accomplished woman. I have worked in the fashion industry my whole adult life and have traveled the world over for both business and pleasure. I have an independent spirit. I have always lived in NYC and still find it amazing; also have an amazing son and daughter-in-law.
LS, sixties, widow

■   ■   ■

Had great relationships that never resulted in marriage and children. Nevertheless, have rich and fulfilling life and hope to meet the man with whom I can share a loving life.
CCC, late sixties, single

■   ■   ■

No pets in bed. As much Botox as I can afford. Also am undergoing physical therapy to cure a bad knee so I can walk and do as much yoga as I like. I'm a

regular girl. I love to do as many good deeds as I can and park my own BMW on the street. OK, it's the Upper East Side. So, what do you think?
BK, early seventies, widow

■ ■ ■

Don't know if you want dual residences in Palm Beach and Manhattan, but just had to say your profile made my day! I laughed out loud. Great sense of humor. Perhaps, not as witty, but always manage to keep friends entertained (and constant chuckling) with stories of love and adventure. (I traveled frequently overseas for business). They say timing is everything...let's just see...
JB, late sixties, widow

■ ■ ■

Wife, mother, teacher, friend. Always interested in my health. No Botox! No facelifts! Physically fit and completely healthy, except for a slight case of arthritis in one knee that doesn't keep me from playing doubles for two hours, once a week. Still do the Times *crossword daily and on Sunday and haven't had to look for my reading glasses since getting that string attachment doodah. We all can't be perfect. Oh, really, truly seventy-four!*
LL, seventy-four, widow

■ ■ ■

A teacher, single mother, but nothing prepared me for this. And though I fear that my wonderful delusion about you and any future we may have might be shattered by introducing reality into the mix, I will muster up my courage to fight my deep trepidation and give you my phone number, as I hope you will do, regardless of your own issues, such as they might be. You can reach me (and please hurry up—that's the other side of my coin) at (---.---.----).
WL, seventies, widow

■ ■ ■

I do love movies and would enjoy them more with another movie-lover. I love black and white films, especially the musicals. I spend my time playing bridge and going to concerts (classical) and plays (on and off Broadway). I have been blessed with a wonderful life that includes a happy marriage, two great children, and a successful career (attorney). Golden years are truly that.
Shirl, seventies, widow

■   ■   ■

No piercings, tattoos, or drugs…simply put, clean. Man of strong character. Confident, secure, upbeat with a great sense of humor. Am happy within myself; I love life to the nth degree. In addition, I am easygoing, I'm comfortable, I'm healthy, and probably one of the happiest men on the planet. It would be nice to hear from you. Your decision. ABOUT LIFE…live it, only one time around…no rehearsals! My philosophy, "unwrap each day as though it were a precious gift."
Jed, seventies, widower

■   ■   ■

My Ideal Relationship/The Kind of Person I'm Looking For

■ ■ ■

We waste time looking for the perfect lover,
instead of creating the perfect love.

—TOM ROBBINS

I BELIEVE I'M a pretty normal guy, and I can't think of a single overriding factor preventing me from wanting to date an attractive woman I found sweet and sincere.

Not so for my friend, Douglas. He has a passion—no—an obsession for the Yankees, and unless his mate demonstrates the same level of dedication, *there is no way we can play ball.* (His words.)

Unfortunately, one must be careful what one wishes for. When Doug finally met a woman who appeared to share his devotion, he took her to a Yankees game. He quickly realized she was one of those rabid fans who not only heckled the opposing team but also their fans. As he told me his story, he asked if I thought him a coward, because after she was showered with beer, instead of going up into the stands as she demanded and defend her honor, he snuck by the row packed with very large and very drunk Red Sox fans and headed for the Exits.

Dare I say it once more? Be careful what you wish for.

■ ■ ■

Don't: Be unrealistic and write *a man who can take "No" for an answer.*

■ ■ ■

Don't: Declare the secret to a good relationship is to *cash in and cash out.*

■ ■ ■

Don't: Be an elitist and ask for someone who knows how to fix a leaky faucet.

■ ■ ■

Don't: Be unrealistic and use *loving, caring,* and *sensitive* in the same sentence.

■ ■ ■

Don't: Be a *fashionista* and ask for a gent who knows how to tie a *full Windsor knot.*

■ ■ ■

Don't: Wish *for anyone who has a phobia* because only *someone who has one could accept yours.*

■ ■ ■

Don't: Say *a guy who has his own plane* because that makes *Frequent Flyers think their miles are useless.*

■ ■ ■

Don't: Say *someone who looks good in a uniform* unless you're willing to break the law and date an *Eagle Scout.*

■ ■ ■

Don't: Raise the bar too high. While you *make fried eggs every* day to remind yourself what your brain looks like on drugs *they just may say "No."*

■ ■ ■

Don't: Think he's insensitive. It's enough he didn't walk out, just don't expect him to have memorized *all of Jack's lines from "Terms of Endearment."*

■ ■ ■

Don't: Use *Donny & Marie* to convince them they're the one. They'll just think, *"A little bit country, A little bit rock and roll,"* is code for a *platonic relationship.*

■ ■ ■

Absolutely Do Not: Use the word *support,* as he could mistake that to mean, you want someone to physically *hold you upright* when you walk.

■ ■ ■

I'm looking for a take-charge kind of man, in case I can't make up my mind. Lol. A man who sweeps me off my feet and takes me to Neverland.
Ellyn, late fifties, divorced

■ ■ ■

To meet a man with a generous spirit—this upbeat blonde radiates poise, grace, and fun. Stylish but not a fashion victim. Reaches out to others. Laughs easily.

Looking for someone who is financially secure, who can enjoy the Manhattan life or Hamptons beach walks!
CP, fifties, divorced

■ ■ ■

Sure, I think she's a horny toad if I find her on different sites. That's why I contact her. Sometimes they use different screen names, posting different photos makes it harder. But when I find them, I'm going to get in touch. That's if she looks good. I mean that's a given.
Mel, fifty, divorced twice

■ ■ ■

Seeking handsome, witty, deftly intelligent, physically fit, successful man for a long-term relationship. Looking for that special person who possesses great dignity and refinement and above all the ability to enjoy life or an inexhaustible Joie de vivre!
Celeste, seventies, widow

■ ■ ■

Right now I am looking to find someone to share experiences with. I am widowed and find I miss being in a committed relationship. I was married young and have three grown children. They are all self-sufficient, married, and have children. If you like my picture and share my interests, please e-mail me. No one from out-of-state, please.
G, sixties, widow

■ ■ ■

I'm a New Yorker who's dressed in black since the sixties, so when an attractive woman who also dresses in all black contacted me I'm interested. We agree to meet for coffee. Not only does she show up dressed in black, she's wearing

matching lipstick, nail polish, and a silver pentagram around her neck. Her skin was so pale and bloodless, as to have the appearance of alabaster. She also had no sense of humor, because when I told her I thought she looked great in colors, she gave me the finger and walked out. Be careful what you wish for!
Steve, midsixties, widower

■ ■ ■

What are important are family, faith, honesty, and respect. Then I believe a sense of humor is necessary if we're to successfully deal with the hardships in life. I also have a desire to let loose sometimes and hope he would be able to show the same kind of spontaneity. Music is magical, and I like to listen to many genres, and dancing can be so romantic. Will send phone number upon request.
Linda L, sixty-five, single

■ ■ ■

For me, kissing a beard or mustache is like kissing a Brillo pad. I make this clear in my profile. So what happens? It's like I challenged every guy with every conceivable type of facial hairs to see if they could convince me to go out with them. You wouldn't believe the lines they feed me. How it makes them more virile. How once you go beard, you'll never go back. Wouldn't be surprised if my profile doesn't wake up Rip Van Winkle and he gets on my case.
FC, fifty-nine, divorced

■ ■ ■

He had a nice face; good sense of humor, and we both had been in the advertising, so I thought he was ideal. We had dinner. Wasn't as cute as his photo, and I thought he'd be funnier. On the plus side, he was a gentleman at the restaurant, and no funny business when he drove me home. An hour later I get his e-mail. A picture of his chest, and when I scroll down—you know—naked down there! With a message that said, "See what you're missing."

When I told my friend Clair, she congratulated me on getting my first set of "Dick Picks."
Ellyn, late fifties, divorced

■   ■   ■

My Perfect First Date

■ ■ ■

When you fall for someone's personality,
everything about them becomes beautiful.

—Reeva Steenhamp

I CAN'T TELL you how many times my mother told me *man plans, god laughs. You shouldn't put all your eggs in one basket* was another of her favorites, when she saw I was setting myself up for teenage heartbreak and needed a reassuring, yet cautionary hug.

Naturally, I never paid her any attention. She was my mother, what could she possibly know? I can see you're nodding in agreement.

It wasn't until I had my *perfect first date* I realized she actually knew what the heck she was talking about.

I'm an avid tennis player, so when I was contacted by a very attractive and interesting woman who loved the game, I thought I've hit the jackpot.

We met up at Starbucks, and she was as lovely and engaging as I imagined. To top it off, she had a summer place with her own court. I was so besotted I threw cost and caution to the wind and bought her a second Frappuccino.

It wasn't until she began to interrogate me that things went south. *Did the ATP give me my ranking, or was it in her words, some rinky-dink tennis club? Did I serve with an American Twist, because her court was Har-Tru, and it was no fun playing with someone who didn't know how to hit a "kick serve."*

It took all my gentlemanly restraint not to kick her out the door!

■ ■ ■

Do: Remember, any mention of *beachy* is code for *buy me something in the Hamptons* and marks you as a *Sling w/Bling* (the summer term for *purse*.)

■ ■ ■

Do: Write *a get-to-know-you walk through the park;* just don't add...*I have a carry permit, so don't worry about muggers.*

■ ■ ■

Don't: Jinx the place by adding...*where my ex-spouse dropped dead.*

■ ■ ■

Don't: Confuse a *perfect* date with *being in perfect condition, that is,* no duel stress tests.

■ ■ ■

Don't: Invite him to try something new because *men are leaders, not followers.*

■ ■ ■

Don't: Declare you won't twist his arm off if he won't dance *the twist,* but know guys that will.

■ ■ ■

Don't: Think exchanging furtive smiles with strangers on a crowded bus *constitutes a first date.*

■ ■ ■

Don't: Write *someone who can hotwire a Corvette* because you've always wanted to steal one and go joy riding.

■　■　■

Don't: Choose a spot where you won't look you're best, that is, any place *young people hang out.*

■　■　■

Don't: Show off your *acting skills* when you're dressed as one of the *three wise men* in the Christmas pageant.

■　■　■

Don't: Say *some out-of-the-way spot,* that is, you've got a boyfriend who'd kill you both if he thought you were stepping out on him.

■　■　■

Don't: Declare *when we look into each other's eyes for the first time and know we've found love...if you're cross-eyed.*

■　■　■

Don't: Pick a rooftop venue; because it's obvious, you'll be using *binoculars to check him out from an adjoining roof.*

■　■　■

Don't: Use *ten-dollar words* when talking to a *five-cent dictionary.* Therefore: *beautiful* is in, *idyllic* is out, and *halcyon*—I don't think so...

■　■　■

Don't: Say...*with me you'll always be ready for anything.* This only reminds him of a *Cialis commercial,* and if he doesn't have ED now, it will give it to him.

■　■　■

Absolutely Do Not: Write *someplace quiet, so you can tell me all about yourself.* Don't you get it—*guys just don't have a lot to say, unless watching sports on TV.*

■　■　■

Perhaps I don't believe there is a perfect first date.
NCB, fifty-nine, divorced

■　■　■

My perfect first date? The last time I have to do this and be disappointed.
LC, fifties, single

■　■　■

Anywhere where the sparks will fly if they're meant to fly.
Jack, fifty, widower

■　■　■

My focus is on you. It would be nice to laugh...humor is important.
Hank, sixty, widower

■　■　■

An instant wow! This could be the right person. Not too much to ask, right?
Terry, seventies, divorced

■　■　■

Perfect? If she would offer to split the check and show we're both in this together. Not that I wouldn't pay.
CP, fifties, divorced

■　■　■

After watching the last one, stare into her coffee for ten minutes, while repeating "awesome," I'd liked someone who didn't bring "funny brownies" to our date.
The Author

■　■　■

When I got home, must have had huge smile because my son, who was visiting that weekend remarked, want to meet this guy! That's when I knew this Internet dating was all worth it! We're married now!
Chris, sixty-seven, divorced

■　■　■

Nothing in life is perfect. Just hope after sizing him up on the phone, he doesn't disappoint. Must live up to my expectations; physically fit, doesn't need me to support him. I'll know from talking to him he has a sense of humor, the smarts to become an engaging partner, and his world view is in sync with mine.
Kay, late fifties, widow

■　■　■

After looking at the photos, the last thing I want is for her to show up looking ten years older and really ugly. It's happened to me and to my friends. The pictures have been retouched. In real life you can see, wrinkles, the double chin. And the facelifts, Botox, and other shit don't hide it. Makes them look

grotesque. But what can you do? Go for someone younger? I don't have the money.
Jack, fifty-nine, widower

■ ■ ■

Coffee house or bar and it must be crowded. No out-of-the way place where he can try some funny stuff. Daytime is a must. Always take your own transportation and try for a place with a valet. I tell all my friends, watch out for the parking lots. Goes without saying, first talk on the phone, make sure it's their home number. Always bring money in case they try to pull a fast one.
Helen, fifties, divorced

■ ■ ■

When my girlfriends and I go on dates or to events held by online dating services, we make it a point to look good. We have a leg wax, hair done, and dress up to fit the occasion. The men come looking like slobs: uncombed hair, unshaven, and looking like they got dressed in the dark. I live in South Florida, so we're always in shorts, t-shirts, but for God sakes, it's not appropriate at a social event, not when you're trying to impress a woman. These guys just don't care.
CP, fifties, divorced

■ ■ ■

This is the wildest, most unusual perfect first date, but here it is. So, my sister just lost her husband and was down in the dumps, so I surprised her by posting her profile online. At first she was mad at me, but when she saw all the men who were sending her e-mails, telling her how much they wanted to meet her, she thanked me. Her first date was with a man we will call Monroe, and because she was new at this, wanted me to be there. Call it serendipity, Kismet,

whatever…but it was love at first sight, the moment we laid eyes on each other. My sister's still angry and tells all our friends how wicked I am and how I stole her boyfriend from her. Monroe says she'll get over it as soon as we get married.
Karen P, late fifties, divorced

■   ■   ■

On My First Date Remind Me to Tell You

■ ■ ■

I'm not trying to be sexy.
It's just my way of expressing myself
when I move around.

—ELVIS PRESLEY

SOMETHING VERY BIZARRE happened when I asked my online vets about this particular question. Each had the very same answer and wanted me to tell readers not to make the same mistake, or they would soon see their dates get up and never return.

What could be so damaging? Simple. *Never, ever* take out your phone and turn up the volume so the entire bar can hear you showing extended videos of your grandchildren! It appears that seeing these innocents take their first steps and then repeatedly falling down and screaming in pain, isn't as humorous as one would think.

I had an entirely different experience. As soon as I got to this question, I remembered the last scene in *Some Like It Hot*. When the Tony Curtis character, that had been pretending to be a girl, confessed to the Joe E. Brown character, "I'm not a woman, I'm a man."

In the film it turns out OK, because Joe E. shyly nods and wisely replies, "Nobody's perfect..."

(Warning! Besides boring a date with home videos, do not confess to any-thing, no matter how innocent and...absolutely...do not think for one second... a first date is the time and place to seek absolution for something really nasty!)

■ ■ ■

Don't: Confess you are more insecure than *Rodney Dangerfield.*

■ ■ ■

Don't: Tell her everyone on your father's side was in *Deliverance.*

■ ■ ■

Don't: Admit unless you're married, *the touch of a man's hand makes you jump.*

■ ■ ■

Don't: Come clean about the *embezzling charge* until you've got something on them.

■ ■ ■

Don't: Confess *you're wired because it's the best way to ensure he never breaks his word.*

■ ■ ■

Don't: Tell them *who shares your bed* until you find out if they're *allergic to alpaca.*

■ ■ ■

Don't: Confess to passing through walls. Not everyone *walks with a zombie in a dream.*

■ ■ ■

Don't: Brag about having a spittoon in every room without first admitting you chew tobacco.

■ ■ ■

Don't: Say anything about the *fortune teller,* until he actually takes you on *a long trip, across the ocean.*

■ ■ ■

Don't: Speak about *Granny's flexibility;* cute as it is, it's scarily similar to Linda Blair's head spin in *The Exorcist.*

■ ■ ■

Don't: Say anything *about going back into Witness Protection* because they might want to vacation in *New Mexico.*

■ ■ ■

Don't: Declare you'd rather have your wisdom teeth extracted than have him explain what *backfield in motion* means.

■ ■ ■

Don't: Show courtroom pictures. You think they prove your innocence, but everyone knows they can be doctored up in *Photoshop.*

■ ■ ■

Don't: Brag *you've beaten the record set by the winner of last year's Hot Dog Eating Contest at Nathan's Famous,* that is, *you're not a sharer.*

■ ■ ■

Don't: Admit nothing's more exhilarating than waking up at 4:00 a.m., looking outside your tent, and seeing *you're first online for the Jimmy Choo winter sale.*

■　■　■

Don't: Retell how you met *Clint Eastwood,* because the short version takes twenty minutes, and the long one—let's just say, *it won't make their day.*

■　■　■

Absolutely Do Not: Leave them hanging by saying…*it has to do with the headless body they found at a certain topless bar.*

■　■　■

How a crane almost fell on my apartment building.
Steve, sixties, divorced

■　■　■

The time I almost ran headlong into a very large hippo.
JJ, midseventies, widow

■　■　■

How can I know that until I know he's worth pursuing?
Helen, fifties, divorced

■　■　■

Tell him what I left out in my e-mails and phone conversations about how good-looking he is. I like to minimize the compliments. Don't want them to go

out with me, because I think they look like Richard Gere. Of course, that's a big reason, but I'm not going to give them a swellhead right off the bat.
Laura, late seventies

■ ■ ■

It was our first date, and we were picking up from our previous conversation about what we collected as kids. On the phone I had told her about my baseball cards, how I stopped when I was a teen but still had a fairly large collection that I'd be leaving for my grandkids. I wanted to tell her how, through my father's connections, I had the opportunity to collect comic books, and had I paid more attention to them, saved them, I'd have a collection worth a fortune. Her face glazed over, and I could see she wasn't listening. She pulled out her phone, shoved it in my face, and showed me photos of her doll collection. Her whole house was filled with 'em: in display cases, on shelves, chairs, tables, beds, hundreds of 'em. It was very impressive, and I asked if she intended to share this amazing collection with the world by one day donating them to a museum. You'd think I stuck a knife in her. She began ranting about how they were living things and that would be like killing 'em. I faked a phone call, got me right out of there. Too bad, she was a stunner.
Steve, early sixties, widower

■ ■ ■

The Things I Could Never Live Without

■ ■ ■

A day without sunshine is like,
you know, night.

—STEVE MARTIN

IN CASE YOU haven't guessed it by now, the questions are becoming more ridiculous! I know, your first response is to throw up your hands and say, *ahh—f-it!*

It was mine. Oh yes! I seriously thought about throwing in the towel and saying this silliness is not worth my time! *I didn't! Instead, I wrote this book so you won't have to!*

The more idiotic the questions seem—the more you must tell yourself; I know your game, I know you are trying to catch me out—but you won't!

Ladies—you will continue to play Madonna's "Material Girl" but instead of confessing that *losing your Cartier Tennis Bracelet is like losing a member of your family,* you'll write: *A summer's sun bathing my face.*

Guys—as much as you'd like to admit *the smell of a beer-soaked barroom floor makes life worth living, you'll write: The aroma of my mom's apple pie on Thanksgiving morning.*

Remember, two can play this game–and you can play it better!

■ ■ ■

Do: Leave out reference to *the South of Fr*ance until you're sure he can afford to stock the chateau with *Domaine de la Romanée-Conti.*

■ ■ ■

Don't: Mention your *nanny*; they'll think you still sleep with your *blankie.*

■ ■ ■

Don't: Mention *multiple passports* until you're sure they *love spy books as much as you do.*

■ ■ ■

Don't: Mention *your love of the water,* that is, *he better have a boat and we're not talking dingy.*

■ ■ ■

Don't: Say *takeout,* that is, *I served my time, and if you want a home-cooked-meal, go live with mommy.*

■ ■ ■

Don't: Refer to your *Johnson.* No vulgarity, no wishful thinking, and *no slang used by your grandchildren.*

■ ■ ■

Don't: List what *you got in the divorce because* when he sees the vanity plate *Mel 1 on the Maserati, he'll know he'll be number 2 until he buys you a Bentley.*

■ ■ ■

Don't: Refer to anything *wooden* or *stuffed.* Who hasn't seen those horror flicks where *toys come alive and kill you?*

■ ■ ■

Don't: Declare the *memory of your first dog* because he'll know every time you *look longingly into his eyes, you're seeing Buffy.*

■　■　■

Don't: Be ashamed of the love you have for your *iPhone, iPad,* or other *mobile devices*; otherwise, he'll think you have no outside interests.

■　■　■

Don't: Say *my angels that were sent from heaven.* In other words, one kid lives next-door, the other across the street, and you'll never have time for him.

■　■　■

Don't: Write *Raindrops on roses and whiskers on kittens, bright copper kettles and warm woolen mittens...*come on—who hasn't seen *The Sound of Music?*

■　■　■

Absolutely Do Not: Write...*LOVE. OMG, OMG*—could you be *less original? Yep...you could answer...MY SMARTPHONE...*

■　■　■

Sarcasm is a cultural imperative.
Helen, fifties, divorced

■　■　■

My A-10 American Shotgun and my 68' Vette.
Harry, eighties, widower

■　■　■

Laughing, movies, a canine pet, my grandson, my independence, and my realism.
Gloria, fifty-five, widow

■　■　■

Friends, family, cats, books, foreign films, and lots and lots of music.
Terry, seventies, divorced

■　■　■

I am looking for someone who will see three movies in a row even if it means changing theaters.
The Author

■　■　■

Must have popcorn while watching movies, even at home (happy to make it).
Karen P, late fifties, divorced

■　■　■

I didn't want to seem too materialistic, so I said family and friends, but what I really wanted to include was my Limoges porcelain collection.
LKS, fifty-nine, single

■　■　■

My wonderful son and his wife, NJ shore, lively conversation w/friends and great martinis! Swimming, biking can't go without them either.
NCB, fifty-nine, widow

■　■　■

Honesty. Definitely honesty. I cannot feel secure in any relationship if I know the guy is lying. One thing getting old age does for you, gives you the ability to see through all bullshit. What's the old saying...if I knew then what I know now?
Helen, fifties, divorced

■ ■ ■

If you're the kind of man who is not afraid of intimacy; If you definitely want to get married and enjoy life; If you are sincere; If the physical is not the most important; If it is what's inside your heart that counts; If you have good intentions and believe truth matter; If you can look the person straight in the eyes; If you want to have a real partner...I will be the one! I want a warm and good life with respect and love...
Linda, sixties, widow

■ ■ ■

I made sure they know how much I love dogs. I even took a picture of me with Toto. Only wrote men who had dogs and loved them as much as I loved mine. Also very important to find out if their dog could get along with mine. Never responded to anyone who didn't have one.
Ellyn, late fifties, divorced

■ ■ ■

My Favorite Books, Movies, TV Shows, Music, and Food

■ ■ ■

Of all the music that reached farthest into heaven,
it is the beating of a loving heart.

—HENRY WARD BEECHER

IF YOU'VE SUFFERED the humiliation that comes from being spotted by your pals when coming out of a movie like *Beaches,* you better not list it as one of your favorites.

Ladies—same with you unless, you're truly addicted to midnight showings of *Fists of Iron.*

Everyone—please check your Netflix cue before you offer to share it with your newly found paramour. My friend, Larry, learned that when a woman writes she doesn't like war movies, finding *Lone Survivor* results in you ending up alone.

Oh—nobody our age takes up *Sanskrit* to improve brain function; so keep to the *Times* Best-Seller list if you must brag about your favorite books of the year.

■ ■ ■

Do: Be realistic. Do you really think that a woman of your age can tolerate the powdered spices of Ethiopian cuisine?

■ ■ ■

Don't: Confess that you rate a movie by the *boxes of tissues you use.*

■   ■   ■

Don't: List *self-help books.* If you can't help yourself, don't expect him to.

■   ■   ■

Don't: Give away any endings, as they may have been saving *House of Cards* for *binge watching.*

■   ■   ■

Don't: Make him think you can't speak English. *"Cage a Folle," "À la Recherché du Temps Perdu,"* and *foie gras…*

■   ■   ■

Don't: Brag you've seen *Hamilton* unless you're going to spend *nine grand on courtside tickets at a Knicks game.*

■   ■   ■

Don't: Instruct him to read anything by *doctors.* He's still angry he had to *wait two hours for a ten minute physical.*

■   ■   ■

Don't: Go with *Terms of Endearment* and *Shogun Assassin* as your all-time faves. They'll only think you're schizoid.

■   ■   ■

Don't: List everything with the same theme, as he might conclude, he'll be the next spouse to *die by arsenic poisoning*.

■ ■ ■

Don't: Mention *Art Houses* to someone who comes from a generation that think you're talking about *Debbie Does Dallas*.

■ ■ ■

Don't: Mention *Hulu*, or any service that doesn't provide live sports, because you'll be flagged for *unsportsmanlike conduct*.

■ ■ ■

Don't: Make a Freudian slip. Come on—*good with a whip* instead of—*good with a whisk*...because you love to make *meringue?*

■ ■ ■

Don't: Brag that after watching the first episode of *Survivor* you had the *coastline of Pulau Tiga tattooed across your shoulder blades.*

■ ■ ■

Absolutely Do Not: Brag you only go to restaurants where you can order *off the menu.* (If you have to ask, imagine his reaction!)

■ ■ ■

A good Chicken Soup...the one I cook.
Helen, fifties, divorced

■ ■ ■

Haggis! His favorite food is Haggis! Ugh!
GGG, sixty-five, widow

■　■　■

The Art of Hearing Heartbeats. A Man called Ove.
SA, fifties, single

■　■　■

Any man that answered they liked to watch Anthony Bourdain's TV show "Parts Unknown" got my attention.
LKS, fifty-nine, single

■　■　■

Don't like to read, but I didn't want to seem illiterate, so I picked the top three books on the NYT Best Seller list.
Mel, fifties, divorced twice

■　■　■

Shark Tank, Tennis, Charlie Rose, Sinatra, opera, classical, NFL, college football, Our Crowd, 40 Chances by Howard Buffett, The End of Greatness By Aaron David Miller.
Harry, eighties, widower

■　■　■

She wrote "The Andrew Sisters." I wasn't sure if she was being nostalgic or just liked their songs. I contacted her, and we've been going out for about a month.

PS: She's seventy-six and I'm seventy-four, and we still dance to "Rum and Coca Cola."
Burt, seventy-four, widower

■ ■ ■

Biographies, memoirs, and fiction...documentaries and foreign films...Curb, PBS, and This Is Us...home cooked meals with family and friends gathered round the table. Any music that feeds the soul or makes us want to dance!
Donna, sixty-eight, divorced

■ ■ ■

If you've seen "Start the Revolution without Me" and nearly choked with laughter we're in sync. Read my profile, scan my photos, and if you like what you see, contact me, and let's go from there
RS, forties, single

■ ■ ■

I'm a big fan of "2000 Year Old Man," love movies (domestic and foreign— sometimes more than one in a day). Love opera and BTW, "Bel Canto" is also the title of a very interesting book by Ann Patchett. I don't have a photo on my site, but I'll be happy to e-mail you one. Take chance—I'm attractive without Botox or surgery! Let's chat.
JJ, midseventies, widow

■ ■ ■

Some women throw in the kitchen sink, no pun intended, to prove they are all things to all men. Every imaginable food they cook, eat: Squid to flapjacks.

Every hit TV show: Gunsmoke to Suits. Oscar award-winning movies: "Double Indemnity" to cult classics like "Freaks." Classic books: Dickens to the latest Michael Connelly. And music! From Gregorian Chants to Calypso. I get dizzy just reading their lists.
Jack, fifty-nine, widower

■　■　■

The Coolest Places I've Visited

■ ■ ■

It is good people who make good places.

—ANNA SEWELL, *BLACK BEAUTY*

NOTHING TURNS ME off more than getting e-mails from women who post photos of themselves in exotic locales. I tell myself, who wants a showoff that poses in front of *The Seven Wonders of the World...in one post*! Give me a break; the exotic bird she's kissing is probably drugged, right?

So—I'm jealous! The truth is—I know these women are unattainable no matter how taken they are with me, because *I can only afford a daytrip to the Jersey Shore.*

Jack, an online vet, told me anyone who writes about a place that only can be reached by dog sleds, traveling across a hundred miles of frozen ice, *has to be frigid; although he confessed he had no actual proof of this, he felt it had to be so.*

Almost all the women I interviewed traveled more than the men. They believed talking about their favorite places and posting pictures of these exciting times, spoke to their sense of adventure.

They thought Jack's reference to their lack of sexual desire moronic; requested his screen name *so they could block his e-mails.*

Perhaps, I'm too bias here and not the right person to critique this question? *Then again, why should I let that stop me, when it hasn't on previous pages?*

■ ■ ■

Do: Understand not everyone thinks wresting crocs and gators is a reason to visit exotic locales.

■ ■ ■

Don't: Brag it doesn't get any better than reading *AARP on the banks of the Nile.*

■ ■ ■

Don't: Declare one really doesn't *get a feel for Bali unless one goes at least four times a year.*

■ ■ ■

Don't: Provide an extensive list of *exotic locales so you can prove you're immune to tropical diseases.*

■ ■ ■

Don't: Bring up the set of *CSI* if you're going to add...*you've always wanted to commit the perfect crime.*

■ ■ ■

Don't: Confess *nothing is more exciting than being right next to the person making your next pair of Prada shoes.*

■ ■ ■

Don't: Say *any place that doesn't have a US Embassy,* that is, if I'm on the lamb, they can't extradite me back to the States.

■　■　■

Don't: List fictional locales like *Middle Earth, Shangri-La,* and *Neverland* no matter how real they appeared in movies.

■　■　■

Don't: Embellish. Just say *Spain.* Leave out *the running with the bulls in Pamplon*a and how you'd love to show him where the *bull gored you.*

■　■　■

Don't: Think this question gives you permission to bring up *past lives* and how fantastic it was *to live at Versailles when you were Marie Antoinette.*

■　■　■

Absolutely Do Not: Say *tombs, crypts, cathedrals,* as they all *spell certain death to your relationship.*

■　■　■

Italy, Italy, Italy. France, Israel, Japan, Budapest!
LC, single, fifties

■　■　■

Soho, The Met, Botanical Gardens, Paris, Rome, Soho, and Venice CA.
Terry, seventies, divorced

■ ■ ■

Over the last ten years, every Super Bowl, World Series, and NBA champion-ship games.
Jack, fifty-nine, widower

■ ■ ■

Traveling is one of my favorite things. I have managed to visit five continents so far, with the Nile and Amazon rivers the most unforgettable.
Melisa, sixty, widow

■ ■ ■

One woman wrote Trinidad because that's where she learned to Limbo. I'm seventy-four and lucky I can bend down to tie my shoe. What is this woman thinking?
BL, seventy-four, widower

■ ■ ■

When a man writes he's retired, has a picture of himself on this gorgeous yacht, and then lists all the exotic islands he's sailed to, naturally, I'm thinking he has money and is someone I want to contact.
CP, fifties, divorced

■ ■ ■

Gun Garage in Vegas! What an experience! Machine Guns! Never thought at sixty-eight I'd have so much fun shooting guns! Have to thank my

son who took me there for my sixty-fifth birthday. Been going back ever since.
Gavin, seventy-two, widower

■ ■ ■

Salmon fishing in Alaska. Snorkeling in Hanauma Bay, Oahu, Hawaii, Cape Ann Whale Watch up in Boston. The Space Show in the Hayden Planetarium at the Rose Center for Earth and Space, NYC. On the back porch with my grandkids.
Thomas, fifty-eight, widower

■ ■ ■

I wrote the local museums in New York City, the Botanical Gardens up in the Bronx and of course Central Park. I just haven't had the good fortune to travel outside of the country, let alone the state. Maybe with someone I meet on the site. That would be nice. But I'm not going to leave it blank just because I can't match up with all the women who have been to places I only can visit on the Travel Channel.
Linda, sixties, widow

■ ■ ■

I write the Florida Keys or maybe ice fishing in Minnesota, but one woman who messaged me said she has been to: Papua New Guinea, Tasmania, Kyoto, Agra, Tanzania, Israel, Botswana, Namibia…First of all, I don't have the money, so does she expect me to go with her? Second, I don't know where half these places are, but by the sound of them, I don't think I want to visit them, so what do we have in common.
Steve, sixties, divorced

■ ■ ■

For Fun I Like To...

■ ■ ■

Life is about using the whole box of crayons.

—RuPaul

If recreational drugs are important, and you want to tell the world about how wasted you got at Woodstock...*don't!*

Even if you can snap a cigarette out of a person's mouth with a bull-whip at fifty paces...*Don't go there, either!*

If ever you're to be ordinary, even boring, this is the time. I will even forgive the banal. Ladies—go ahead and write: *I just love watching the sun slowly set over the water. Guys—go ahead and be totally unoriginal and confess: There's nothing better than playing catch in the backyard with my grandchild.*

OK, so we all have a little of the Walter Mitty in us; but for now, on this dating site, *keep the snake charming on the down-low until you know they'll wear a turban and accompany you on the flute.*

■ ■ ■

Do: Share. So you love a *crime scene, but not everyone likes to pull fibers out of a bloodstained carpet.*

■ ■ ■

274

Don't: Say *a walk in space when the park is more practical.*

■ ■ ■

Don't: Be naïve to think everybody likes to *throw water balloons off terraces.*

■ ■ ■

Don't: Lie and say it's *Jell-O* when it's *mud wrestling gets your juices to flow.*

■ ■ ■

Don't: Declare *hiking until you're sure he has the stamina to pick up his clothes.*

■ ■ ■

Don't: Admit *talking in a squeaky voice. They may want helium for blowing up balloons.*

■ ■ ■

Don't: Confess when *feeling unappreciated you walk by construction workers hoping they'll whistle.*

■ ■ ■

Don't: Think because it's for charity, they'll join you in *The Climb to the Top. The Empire State Building? Really?*

■ ■ ■

Don't: Declare your passion is the *Throwing the Maidens off the Cliff Pageant* without knowing if they're afraid of heights.

■ ■ ■

Don't: Admit it's spending an *entire day admiring your shoes because he'll think there won't be any closet space left for him.*

■ ■ ■

Don't: Say *crashing weddings until they beg you to play the accordion, unless you're looking for a partner with a trained monkey.*

■ ■ ■

Don't: Declare *at the drop of a hat, you love jumping into fountains, without knowing he also likes to take his clothes off in public.*

■ ■ ■

Don't: Proclaim I*'m ready for everything* and then ask…*Are you?* You're going on a date, not participating in an episode of *Survivor*.

■ ■ ■

Don't: Say *pretending you don't speak English when foreigners ask directions* because he knows, you'll do it to him when he wants a beer from the fridge.

■ ■ ■

Don't: Confess to *buying expensive clothing, wearing them once, then returning them. That's twice he'll have to go shopping with you!*

■ ■ ■

Absolutely Do Not: Declare meeting *eligible prospects at funerals. You always need to keep one ace up your sleeve.*

■ ■ ■

Play like a little girl. I am full of dreams! And I like to make crazy things!
Ellyn, late fifties, divorced

■ ■ ■

I have an old racecar that I have had for twenty-two years and enjoy working on.
Jack, fifty-nine, widower

■ ■ ■

Golf, but stopped since I couldn't stand people watching me land in the water or sand. It's a real head game.
Harry, eighties, widower

■ ■ ■

Write, go to theatre, movies, concerts, lectures, Morikami gardens, good conversation with friends, dance, belly laugh, etc, etc, etc.
Melissa, sixties, widow

■ ■ ■

One woman wrote she loved Jane Austin, attended some kind of weekend where they all dressed up like her. I think that was it? Sounded nutty. She was very attractive, but I figure she was too strange for me.
Gavin, seventy-two, widower

■ ■ ■

Movies! I saw "Volver" (I've seen everything by Almodovar), and "The Last King" is on my hit list. Not sure about "The Fountain." The Times and the New Yorker didn't like it. Saw "The Departed" because I had to see Leonardo, Matt Damon, and Mark Wahlberg together with my own eyes.
Chris, sixty-seven, divorced

■ ■ ■

I watch out for collectors. Anyone who likes weird stuff like collecting antique sewing thimbles, I've seen that one. I'm not kidding. You can't believe what women my age have been collecting since the sixties. They even talk about traveling all over the country, even Europe to lay their hands on this stuff.
Jackie, sixties, single

■ ■ ■

I like to go to theater, opera, and ballet. I love to go to fun new restaurants, but like to entertain at home. I like going for long walks in the city, and at the beach. I love to spend time with good friends. I also like to stay home, read a good book, watch a good movie, and light a fire in my fireplace.
Beth, fifties, single

■ ■ ■

Another section where people put down every single little thing. I just wish they would use a little judgment. One guy wrote he liked to restore old cars and described in detail how he found the old parts and got the car back to its original self. Who cares? Another one listed all the World Series games he's attended since 1954. I just wrote Broadway Shows and museums. I could have listed every show I've seen since 1960, all the museum exhibitions, even the ones in Europe. I didn't. Come on, have a little restraint.
Helen, fifties, divorced

■ ■ ■

What Is Your Favorite Thing About the Summer

■ ■ ■

Summer means happy times and good sunshine.
It means going to the beach,
going to Disneyland, having fun.

—BRIAN WILSON

THIS QUESTION ALMOST made me fib. Instead of answering truthfully and heaven knows, I do a lot of fun things in the summer, I was transported back to my youth and almost wrote... *Body surfing. Listening to the Drifter's latest hits on my transistor radio. Having all the girls admire my twenty-eight inch waist.*

I'm not the only one to get lost in sauce. Eyes glazed over and become completely unfocused when I broached this subject to fellow boomers and I could tell they were going down the same road.

While we all have wonderful memories of being *The Boys and Girls of Summer, we now must be realistic and cannot* write *skinny-dipping unless your entire body's been frozen in place with Botox.* More to the point, anything that requires you to expose vast portions of your aging epidermis should be avoided. This is especially true for men who still see *Charles Atlas* in the mirror, while the rest of us see the *Pillsbury Doughboy.*

And ladies—*be wary of using the schmaltz.* The *Shallow Hals* of the world will take any reference to sunrises and sunsets to mean you're a nymphomaniac and have to have sex from morning to night. *(They also happen to be the primary buyers of ED medications.)*

Not to worry. No Summers of Discontent for you, dear reader—only ones filled with sunshine and fun!

■   ■   ■

Don't: Steal song lyrics. If he sees another, "Summertime and the livin is easy," he's going to get heat stroke.

■   ■   ■

Don't: Declare it's *your love of the water.* In other words, *he better have a boat, and we're not talking canoe.*

■   ■   ■

Don't: Boast *how you look younger, more beautiful with a tan* when it's common knowledge, everybody does!

■   ■   ■

Don't: Say how much you love *nude beaches* until you can visualize him putting up a *beach umbrella, in his birthday suit.*

■   ■   ■

Don't: Be hypocritical and talk about *six-pack abs gleaming in the sun, when you'd call him a dirty old man for wanting the same.*

■   ■   ■

Don't: Write *blackouts* because that's when you get to stay at your sister's mansion in Amagansett and she can't do a thing about it.

■   ■   ■

Don't: Declare *riding with the top down, listening to seventies' gold* when he's just *scaled down, sold his car, and given up his Sirius subscription.*

■ ■ ■

Don't: Think this question permits you to write *arm and arm through a field of wild flowers—trite is trite; boring is boring, whatever the season.*

■ ■ ■

Don't: Confuse honesty with unburdening your soul. Thoughts of strangling men who'd rather watch baseball than go antiquing are best left unsaid.

■ ■ ■

Absolutely Do Not: Say *fake a drowning* so *young, muscular lifeguards* will rescue you, and if you play it right, *give you mouth-to-mouth resuscitations.*

■ ■ ■

I have a friend who wrote she hated the summers because she got skin rashes from the sun, the sand, watermelons, and looked overweight in a bathing suit. You wonder why no guy contacted her, even though she's really very attractive. Steve, early sixties, widower

■ ■ ■

Walking on the beach listening on my transistor radio to: "Bye By Love" by the Everly Brother, "Searchin'" by the Coasters, "Short Fat Fannie" by Larry Williams and, of course, the aforementioned Drifters. How come I can remember them but not where I put my reading glasses? The Author

■ ■ ■

On Friday and Saturday
Nights I Typically...

■ ■ ■

It's 4:58 on Friday afternoon.
Do you know where your margarita is?

—AMY NEFZGER

WANT TO KILL myself...
Quit whining!
But that's how I feel sometimes...
Stop feeling sorry for yourself.
But...But...
This section is the big kahuna!
I didn't know...
What you say now will make or break you. You go into that dark place now...It's binge-watching "Breaking Bad" for the rest of your sad life.
What should I do?
Continue being strong. You're almost at the end of the profile! Put that smile back on your face and lighten up!

■ ■ ■

Don't: Confuse *trolling* for *strolling* down the avenue.

■ ■ ■

Don't: Lament no *Early Bird Specials* on the weekend.

■　■　■

Don't: Admit that the *weekend is a time to let loose with Vicks VapoRub and Bengay.*

■　■　■

Don't: Reveal *you'd be having one hell of a time, if it weren't for your damn hip.*

■　■　■

Don't: Be boringly unoriginal and write *looking for love in all the wrong places.*

■　■　■

Don't: Confess *how being a third wheel makes you want to put your head on the third rail.*

■　■　■

Don't: Declare *you spend Saturday nights dancing alone in the dark to Barry White tunes.*

■　■　■

Don't: Say *talking to yourself in the mirror because it's more entertaining than meeting men in bars.*

■　■　■

Don't: Admit it's time to use your *second best opening line: "Come on—how many face-lifts do you think I've had?"*

■ ■ ■

Don't: Declare how you *love to let it all hang out.* Obviously, you mean *go wild;* unfortunately, he's visualizing your *flabby arms and bulging belly.*

■ ■ ■

Absolutely Do Not: Admit it's time to use your *best opening line…Are you good with a whip?*

■ ■ ■

Usually, I've lined up a date. I'm on a fixed income, so I'll meet them for Happy Hour. I find out beforehand what they like to drink. If it's martinis, I know a place where even at Happy Hour they're not twenty bucks.
Lauren, sixty-one, divorced

■ ■ ■

Tuesdays and Fridays are Happy Hour. I have three girlfriends I go with. We have our special places from Hollywood to Boynton Beach.
CP, fifty, divorced

■ ■ ■

Every day is Saturday night when you're retired. I'd rather stay home and beat the maddening crowds and go out during the week. I like jazz clubs and wish there were more here.
Gavin, seventy-two, widower

■ ■ ■

I make things up. I'm not going to confess I'm home alone. I certainly don't go on the computer and let the world know I'm by myself. I write, you know, the typical things: movies, plays, concerts, and friends. Never bars or singles events, that also makes you look desperate. Obviously, I know this is an important question, so you both can discover if you're compatible, but for women like me who are ashamed we've been without a mate for a longtime, this is a very painful question.

FC, fifty-nine, divorcee

■ ■ ■

How Do You Prefer to Listen to the News

■ ■ ■

In the case of news,
we should always wait
for the sacrament of confirmation.

—VOLTAIRE

I ADMIT, I thought this one of the more bizarre questions. My darker, more suspicious side, wondered if they were really inquiring into my physical or mental well-being.

In other words, did they want me to admit I needed to be intoxicated because the news is generally so bad and anxiety producing, no sober person can get through it? (My first *Don't*).

Then I thought, because of the *Internet and Social Media,* traditional outlets like TV and newspapers have become so outdated, the site simply wanted to find out how modern a guy I was.

I asked a few online vets, and they thought I was off my rocker, until I showed them the actual question. They didn't remember it, or if they had, had no recollection as to their reply.

I don't have to alert the news junkies and political wonks that watch *the Senate Floor webcasts* because I know you take this question seriously. For the rest of us, continue to have some patience, follow my advice and lastly…good night and good luck.

■ ■ ■

Don't: Be *un-American and say the BBC.*

■ ■ ■

Don't: Be *un-American* (again) and say on *the telly.*

■ ■ ■

Don't: Be *mystical* and confess *through my crystal ball.*

■ ■ ■

Don't: Display your *inability to concen*trate and reply, *tweets.*

■ ■ ■

Don't: Proclaim *with a drink in my hand, preferably a double.*

■ ■ ■

Don't: Show your *age and respond CBS because I love Walter Cronkite.*

■ ■ ■

Don't: Declare by *bullhorn when the cops come looking for the bad guys.*

■ ■ ■

Don't: Say *the wireless* unless you want to hook up with a *foreign agent.*

■ ■ ■

Don't: Show your love of beards and *declare CNN because Wolf Blitzer is hot.*

■   ■   ■

Don't: Say my *next-door neighbor,* even if they call her, the *Mayor of seventy-second street.*

■   ■   ■

Don't: Declare *the trending section on Facebook,* unless you're ready to date a millennial.

■   ■   ■

Don't: Say *I'm a visual person.* In other words, *you won't get the picture, unless he draws you one.*

■   ■   ■

Don't: Brag while head down, *listening on your news app, as you crash into anyone who gets in your way.*

■   ■   ■

Don't: Say on your *convertible's radio; top down, wind blowing in your face, mouthing out the announcer's words.*

■   ■   ■

Absolutely Do Not: Say *this is the dumbest f-ing question,* and *I refuse to answer it!* (I know, by this time you've lost all patience and are really to give up. Don't!)

■   ■   ■

I'm old school. I like the papers, and I like to go out and get 'em every morning. Like the joke goes, go straight to the obituaries, make sure my name's not there.
Mel, fifties, divorced twice

■ ■ ■

On my smartphone. I get updates from CNN. Very cool. Oh, and I make sure to turn my phone off when I'm on a date, not like some of my girlfriends.
Laura, late sixties, widow

■ ■ ■

My Past Relationships

■ ■ ■

Every new beginning comes
from some other beginning's end.

—SENECA

WHEN I GOT to this question, I had to get up from the computer, walk to the open window, and take a deep breath. I had not dated since my divorce and certainly didn't want to discuss my previous marriage. I would write the standard, yet dodgy response—*will tell you later.*

I was spared further anxiety when I looked out onto the East River and saw a huge commuter ferry pass. I smiled. The ship reminded me, of my neighbor Kenny, and his online tale of woe.

About a year ago, Kenny thought he found his true love on a dating site. She checked all the boxes, and *for the first several months of their relationship, everything was magical.* (His words.)

I know Kenny for years, and it was completely in keeping with his magnanimous personality that, in a gesture of goodwill, he decided to treat Barbara, and her mother Hilde, to a cruise to Bermuda.

They left from New York, and after a blissful one-day journey, safely reached their idyllic destination. Moments after docking, the ship's captain and two security officers came to his cabin. The officers quickly searched it, as Kenny stood by, alarmed and perplexed. This distress, however, did not match the shock of seeing them open Barbara's huge steamer trunk to reveal hundreds of breakfast and dinner rolls. Before he could utter a word, the captain opened the adjoining door to Hilde's cabin. Both Barbara and her mom were sitting on the bed, holding hands, as another security officer stood next to an open refrigerator crammed full of tiny gold packets of butter.

What is really amazing is Kenny posted the story on his site and immediately was inundated with women sympathetic to his plight.

Since then, he's not had a weekend without a date, although he did confess, he still flinches when a waitress comes over and asks if he wants some bread and butter for the table.

■　■　■

Don't: Be secretive and declare *that's between my hairdresser and me.*

■　■　■

Don't: Take the question literally and say the *first person to give you a hicky.*

■　■　■

Don't: Recall how *happy they were right up until the end.* Are you saying *you killed them with love?*

■　■　■

Don't: Rehash *the divorce settlement* and give your new paramour ideas on how they can screw you, too.

■　■　■

Don't: Announce *soon to become a major motion picture* without assuring them they'll be your date at the premier.

■　■　■

Don't: Declare *what's past is prologue.* Come on, do you really believe he's capable of understanding that concept?

■   ■   ■

Don't: Reply *none of your beeswax.* If you're going to be snarky, be an adult and say—*f-you and the horse you rode in on!*

■   ■   ■

Don't: Go into *what ifs.* Code for *regrets.* Just give it up and make certain you make your new love takes a *lie detector test.*

■   ■   ■

Don't: Hash over your regrets. For example, not giving him a *lie detector test when you suspected he was on a honeymoon.*

■   ■   ■

Don't: Link to the episode on *Judge Judy* where *she got your ex-spouse to give you the cash in his Cayman Island's bank account.*

■   ■   ■

Don't: Go on about how *life without your ex-spouse isn't worth living.* So why didn't you throw yourself into the grave with him or her?

■   ■   ■

Absolutely Do Not: Declare *I like my women with fava beans and a good Chianti.*

■   ■   ■

No man wants to hear about failed marriages or husbands dying unexpectedly from rare diseases or car crashes. That's why I leave out any sad stuff and only talk up the happy times.
Burt, seventy-eight, widower

■　■　■

I am a widower and was happily married for thirty years. The success of my marriage has propelled me to try and find a loving and empowering relationship going forward.
Gavin, seventy-two, widower

■　■　■

Have learned that you need to have a good rapport with that person and they have to have respect for the other person's feelings; listening to one another is important, having trust and good communication.
Beth, fifties, single

■　■　■

I have been very fortunate. Two, long and happy marriages that unfortunately ended in their untimely passing. I'm hoping to be as lucky on the Internet. One month in and several prospects...
GGG, sixty-five, widow

■　■　■

It's not all the exotic places you've visited or lived; nor is it your bucket list of faraway locales you must explore before you pass. It is the here and now with someone you love and cherish and who reciprocates in kind.
LKS, fifty-nine, single

■　■　■

I normally don't look at anything but their photos, but sometimes I read this section, and nothing turns me off more than when they write about how happy their marriage was and how perfect their children turned out. I don't have anything in common with someone like that.
Mel, fifties, divorced twice

■   ■   ■

Psychological Questions

■ ■ ■

He who knows others is wise;
he who knows himself is enlightened.

—LAO TZU

NOW YOU'VE DREDGED up past relationships, and either are hopelessly depressed you'll never find another true love like your dearly departed, or you can't find a way of departing your ex-spouse from this world without going to prison…it's time to play…*Psych-out the Prospect!*

One online vet shared this e-mail message, asked me what I thought it meant, and how he should respond to it.

I wish you would be a little bit more direct and tell me how you really feel or else please up your medication. What's your phone number as I don't think this medium is conducive to making dreams (however delusional) come true unless you're an undercover policeman pretending to be a woman pretending to be man who is really…oh damn, I lost my train of dementia.

I had no answer, other than to privately thank my luck stars I didn't get this communiqué.

Another vet shared a message she sent, informing me, that so far, no man has provided a satisfactory reply.

If Men are from Mars and Women from Venus, what planet would Freud chose for his office?

Naturally, she was trying to psych me out; I did a mind-meld and calmly replied, *none—he'd be making "couch calls."* Ba-dum-bum-CHING!

■　■　■

Don't: Be totally honest and reply *you're too depressed to answer.*

■　■　■

Don't: *Play shrink.* Do not throw the questions back into questioners' face.

■　■　■

Don't: Become defensive and use profanity—*nobody's questioning your sanity.*

■　■　■

Don't: Declare your *favorite male trait is submission* unless you're on an S&M site.

■　■　■

Don't: Reply *getting a Rolex* on graduation, when asked *what you cherished most about high school.*

■　■　■

Don't: Say *your favorite childhood memory is gouging the eyes out of wooden puppets.*

■　■　■

Don't: Embellish. When recalling your precious *teddy*, no need to add... *that I stole from a blind girl in the playground.*

■　■　■

Don't: Write the first thing that comes into your head: For example: *I've never loved cats, because they're so freaking independent.*

■　■　■

Don't: Mention how you look forward to dreaming about famous dead people. I understand it's something you've always done, but that doesn't make it normal.

■　■　■

Absolutely Do Not: Use your Rorschach test as proof *the devil's in the ink spots.*

■　■　■

I got off one site because their answers sounded like those you read in astrological reading sites or in a Chinese fortune cookie.
Cal, fifties, divorced twice

■　■　■

I'm no shrink, but nobody has the right, especially the way you look to be so arrogant as to speak, so degrading and negatively stereotypical toward women. I'm surprised someone has not reported you.
Name withheld (sent to author)

■　■　■

I found him. He was cute. Liked his essay. No red flags. E-mailed him. Had interesting and flirtatious exchanges. He worked in the same field, shared experiences. He called; we talked for over an hour, even though I wanted to keep it short and sweet. Was taken with him, so I decided to meet him. Usually, I insist on coffee but had such an entertaining time on the phone, agreed when he suggested dinner. He was extremely charming, and we had a lovely dinner. In the parking lot, we kissed goodnight. He drove off, but I was too enchanted by the kiss to start up and drive away. It was then I received a text message indicating he'd like to start having phone sex. You tell me, where were the psychological questions that pointed to him being a sex fiend?

A, seventy-three, widow

■ ■ ■

You Should Definitely Message Me If You...

■ ■ ■

I'm warning you, if you take one step closer,
I'm never letting you go.

—ADAM, *NO STRINGS ATTACHED*

AN ONLINE VETERAN confided this was one of the more difficult questions to answer. She wanted to respond truthfully by saying b*ecause you find me desirable,* but by doing so, thought *she was baring her soul and becoming much too vulnerable to strangers.*

Guys I interviewed were cool and laid-back, carelessly so, in some cases. (Remember Shallow Hal?)

One guy said he took on the *Popeye Persona* with the motto: *"I Yam What I Yam & Dats What I Yam!"*

What should your response be? My advice? *Somewhere in between over the rainbow and it's all rock and roll, baby.*

■ ■ ■

Do: *Think I'm sexy? If Rod Steward can sing it, you can say it.*

■ ■ ■

Do: *Want to have sex;* but omit *in a pew at midnight mass,* if you're on a religious site.

■ ■ ■

Do: Share my despair and hopelessness now that *Downton Abbey* is over.

■ ■ ■

Do: *Want to get naked on beaches,* but add…*lay bare-ass on bearskin rug*s. He might be an indoor kinda-guy.

■ ■ ■

Do: *Believe Elvis is alive.* Just don't make *seeing him a condition.* Not every-one's been lucky enough to bump into him at the 7-Eleven.

■ ■ ■

Don't: "*Want a piece of me?*" Unless you feel lucky…"*Do you feel lucky, punk?*"

■ ■ ■

Don't: *Are hung like a rhino.* (Remember what I said—*be careful what you wish fo*r.)

■ ■ ■

Don't: *Love in all the wrong places.* So that's your history, but *two wrongs won't get you, Mr. Right.*

■ ■ ■

Don't: *Get any answer right on the compatibility checklist.* You have to draw the line somewhere.

■ ■ ■

Don't: *Like walking along the railroad tracks*. He might think you're suicidal and not a fan of *Some Kind of Wonderful*.

■   ■   ■

Don't: *Believe slow dancing leads to an unwanted pregnancy*. Remember, that may have been something you believed in thirty years ago.

■   ■   ■

Absolutely Do Not: Have to submit a Dun & Bradstreet credit report. Don't want to shoo away guys who have money in an offshore account.

■   ■   ■

Don't be shy. Life is an adventure full of chances. Take a chance on love.
Terry, seventies, divorced

■   ■   ■

Big METS fan with great season tickets. Not that I want to bribe you...
LOL..
Hank, sixties, widower

■   ■   ■

What a cutie. Want to hang out? Say in Central Park by the Bethesda
Fountain?
Paula, seventy, divorced

■   ■   ■

Looking for companionship with someone special—a best friend, and big hugs and kisses. Enjoy!
KSK, single

■ ■ ■

Yes, yes, yes to all your questions! For anything else you will just have to ask me, I have nothing to hide, so just ask.
LS, sixties, widow

■ ■ ■

I am writing to you because your profile suggests you've been looking in the wrong places. Not all women are like that. There are women who are centered, adjusted and happy with themselves, have created wonderful lives for themselves, and just want to share some of that joy. Are you up to the challenge?
A, seventy-four, widow

■ ■ ■

I'm told I'm a nice guy. Easygoing, active on a daily basis and open to new experiences. Your profile indicates these are the characteristics you are looking for in a partner. As we both originally come from the Midwest, I think this is another important indication we share a common history and values.
Name withheld (sent to Donna, sixty-eight, divorced)

■ ■ ■

Here are my top-ten reasons to contact me.

1. *I am slim and fit.*
2. *I am warm and caring.*
3. *My photos are real and recent.*
4. *I love animals and people in that order.*

5. *I had been married for a long time, and I know how to communicate and compromise.*
6. *I am intelligent. I am studying for my Bat Mitzvah in May.*
7. *I am a lousy typist.*
8. *I am taking golf lessons.*
9. *I make the best chocolate-chip cookies on the East Coast.*
10. *I am unique. There is only one of me on the shelf. I will be sold soon, so will you bite the bullet and contact me? You won't be sorry.*

Name withheld (sent to The Author)

■ ■ ■

I simply "must" communicate with you because you rescued me today…I was sooo sad Nora Ephron died, until I read your hilarious essay on unacceptable personality traits. Please let me know if you can live with the following:

1. *Yes, I have one pair of Manolos, 2" heel, gift from a girlfriend, only wear them in the apartment.*
2. *Only one Maltese 7 1/2 lbs., in the bed sometimes.*
3. *I'm the only Jewish woman who abhors shopping, but I love to open the closet door and have the nice stuff in there.*
4. *Hate Jell-O or anything else gelatinous.*
5. *My answering machine says "right woman, wrong time, please leave a message."*
6. *I have played golf and love it—don't have a partner.*
7. *I use my Metro Card twice daily.*

If you think you can overlook any or all of my personality flaws, please respond—I would really enjoy hearing from you!
Name withheld (sent to The Author)

■ ■ ■

Going Live

■ ■ ■

Kilgore: How're you feeling, Jimmy?
Door Gunner: Like a mean motherfucker, sir!

—*APOCALYPSE NOW*

CONGRATULATIONS! YOU HAVE followed my *Dos*, avoided the *Don'ts*, created a picture-perfect profile without stressing out too much. (Hey, don't get down on yourself; nobody does it without a drink or two.)

Now it's game time. Take a deep breath. Press the *submit button*—and as they say in the web biz—*Go live!*

Hold it! Don't press that button!

I almost let you step into the dark hole known as cyberspace, without taking you behind the scenes and showing you how dating sites employ sophisticated and propriety programming to find you your perfect mate.

So here's the skinny. A cupid leaves the *land of love and enchantment* and flies through the Ether into your device, affixes your profile to his arrow, returns, dips the arrow into the *Waters of Algo Rithms, zooms back up, and guided by the magic elixir, shoots the arrow into your lover's device, and* voilà…you both live happily ever after. Admit it, doesn't that reassure you? Now, aren't you ready to—*Go Live!*

■ ■ ■

I was nervous and needed a friend. Why not get support when you need it?
Ellyn, late fifties, divorced

■　■　■

Like riding a bike. Once you learn how, you never forget. Been on and off sites for nearly five years.
KK late fifties widow

■　■　■

He must have a great voice. That worried me the most. Going online, then talking to him on the phone.
Nan, fifty-nine, divorced

■　■　■

I learned the hard way. The best way to show you're not interested is never answer e-mails. Once you do, you're setting up a conversation; so unless you're attracted to the person, want to get to know him or her, ignore his or her messages.
Steve, early sixties, widower

■　■　■

Option One: They Make the First Move

■ ■ ■

Something's wrong with my eyes,
I can't take them off your photo.

—ANONYMOUS

LADIES—REMEMBER *SHALLOW Hal, Cautious Hal, and Substance Man?*
Unfortunately, the algorithms dating sites employ do not distinguish between
them, so your profile will likely be distributed among them, equally. (Ugh!)

Two things happen when a guy opens your profile. *He eyes your photo*
and looks to see if there's a "New Member" sticker.

(Warning! Newbies are like blood in the water to sharks.)

Two things happen when a woman opens your profile. She eyes your
photo, but wants to know more and will go to your essay.

Got the difference? Men…Are you listening!

So—you like the profile. You will send a message. Either it will contain
a personal expression of interest or a standardized message created by the
site called, *A Flirt.*

(A second warning! Flirts are for the lazy, the dullard, and you must never,
ever respond to them, or you use them.)

Be aware, as your profile pops up in their inbox, the profiles the site
chooses for you, will pop up in your inbox. (Heaven be praised, you should
be so lucky that the two match!)

So—boys and girls, now it's simple a question of how you are going to
handle your success. Read on boomers—read on.

■ ■ ■

Noticed (XXX) has a three-course dinner special with wine till 6:30 for $11.95, a touch of Boca Raton in our backyard. Are you up for it latter part of the week?
SA, fifties, single

■　■　■

Thank you so much for the time spent reading your clever and hysterical profile. I am extremely grateful my bathroom is so close to the computer...laughter does that to women sometimes.
Helen, fifties, divorced

■　■　■

Your tardiness is forgiven (what tardiness?) but how can I send a photo without an e-mail address? I am not a computer maven, but even I know an address is required. I am going out now, but I'll check my messages later when I return.
HG, seventy-four, widow

■　■　■

No coffee dates, only dinner. I always pick the place and make sure to tell them upfront there's a dress code. If they don't like that, I don't go. I have been accused of being someone only after a free dinner, but I've been called worse by my ex-husband.
Fran, midsixties, divorced

■　■　■

Thank you for checking out my non-Botoxed pictures and remarking that you found me attractive. I am also happy you complimented my figure and noticed how well I kept in shape. I see by your photos you are also one who works out on a daily basis.
Gloria, fifty-five, widow

■　■　■

It was nice talking to you. I am looking forward to Sat. If there's something you would like to do, it would be fine. I'm sorry I suggested the movie; I have a habit of expressing my thoughts out loud.
FC, fifty-nine, divorced

■　■　■

My best line when I'm with a new date. I'll tell you. I look around the room, point out the people on their phones, then I take mine out and make a big deal out of the fact I've turned it off. I then go into my spiel. "I'm with you. I'm not going to let anyone or anything thing distract me." Works every time.
CP, fifties, divorced

■　■　■

He sent me three e-mails before I finally responded. I wasn't crazy about his picture. Actually, he was balding, and I don't like guys without a full head of hair. The first e-mail was just a "hi." We have a lot in common, and I liked the fact you've done a lot of traveling. The second and third e-mails talked about some of the trips he's taken to places I loved—the Greek Islands for one and some of the Baltic Countries. The face that he loved to cruise was another plus. I guess it was also his persistence. We've been dating exclusively now for the last year.
Linda, sixties, widow

■　■　■

You Respond to Their E-mail

■ ■ ■

He drew me like gravity.

—M. Leighton, *For the Love of a Vampire*

There's nothing like getting that first message. Some ladies have told me they've opened up a bottle of *the bubbly and danced around the room like it's 1984.* (Thanks Prince, for that one.)

Don't think men don't get equally excited. I actually thought about some chest bumping; only I was alone and didn't think the wall would be an appropriate partner.

The Shallow Hals I interviewed confessed to actually believing they were being propositioned and immediately ran to their local pharmacies to get an additional supply of ED meds.

Oh—and while we're talking about doing the dirty, I did have one woman tell me she went out and spent a thousand dollars on lingerie at a place called, *Agent Provocateur.* (I've visited the place, and although the woman didn't tell me how the date went, it wasn't a matter of *if,* but *how quickly* he became putty in her hands.)

So—what to do now?

First—*enjoy the moment—Responsibly!* You've earned it. You've followed my advice and gotten results, but after that *moment,* and I say *Moment*—it's time to return to earth and get serious again. That means continuing on to the next section and get to the business of answering their e-mails—*Responsibly!*

(*Warning! I hate repeating myself, but this must be pounded into your noggin! Until you meet them, and decide for yourself they are not the kind to wear*

309

a Donald Duck rubber mask to a bank…never, ever…reveal any personal info.)

■   ■   ■

Yes, let's meet for coffee and look in each other's eyes and talk.
RS, forties, single

■   ■   ■

Age hasn't slowed me down. I like trains, planes, and automobiles; the faster the better. Contact me if you have the need for speed.
Gavin, seventy-two, widower

■   ■   ■

Your letter is witty and charming. Would like to know more about you. My phone number is (---) (---) (----). Call anytime. Anything is possible.
Karen P, late fifties, divorced

■   ■   ■

This is the first time I've done something like this! I am also a great movie fan. It seems we have many interests in common. I live in the city and love it. I haven't posted my picture yet. I'm 5'2, 120 lbs, physically fit and, I'm told, attractive. Maybe I'll hear from you?"
Shirl, seventies, divorced

■   ■   ■

If I have learned the art of reading this site, I believe you are what is amusingly described as a Secret Admirer. If not, you have my apologies. Perhaps if I, too, may be allowed to "cut to the chase," let me say your laundry list enumerates personality demands and that, my dearest of friend, is not what touches our

hearts. The heart cares not for such superficial demands. It is essence not personality that loves—if love we can.
Gloria, fifty-five, widow

■　■　■

What gets my attention? Sure an attractive woman, and I can't deny I'm a sucker for cleavage, but I like to travel; so if she's written something really cool along those lines, I'm going to contact her no matter what she looks like. Let me give you for instance. "I lived with Tibetan nomads at 17,000 ft. altitude and chased one-horned rhinos on elephant back in game preserves in India, with my telephoto lens." Now, who wouldn't write that person back?
Jack, fifty-nine, widower

■　■　■

l liked what you had to say, and am happy to reply that I am nothing like what you described in your profile. I am quite real and unpretentious, have a zest for life, am romantic and am seeking that "special" someone to love. I feel there is nothing greater than being with the one you can't live without. Of course, I do feel, at times, everyone needs their own space. I might add that I love Manhattan and all it has to offer, especially the arts, for which I have a passion, and I love the West Village, Soho, the Upper West Side, Lincoln Center, and so on. You are someone whom I would like to get to know, because you sound very interesting and bright. Take care, enjoy the week ahead, and I do hope we touch base very soon and that you decide to call.
Linda, sixties, widow

■　■　■

Review Their Compatibility Checklist

■ ■ ■

What counts in making a happy marriage
is not so much how compatible you are
but how you deal with incompatibility.

—LEO TOLSTOY

LET ME TELL you what happens when you don't take this section seriously. I was still blowing into my steaming cup of coffee with two dollops of whip, when I felt her looking me over, as she purposely stirred her Mocha Frappuccino. Then, as if suddenly deciding I passed some sort of test, she smiled and softly asked, "If I ever dressed up during sex...you know like an animal?"

Because my profile displayed my sense of humor, I thought she was giving me a comic opening, so I quipped, *only when I'm alone.*

The smile was beginning to spread across my face, and had I not been so full of myself for coming up such a witty rejoinder, I would have noticed her expression morphing into the face in Edvard Munch's *The Scream.*

Now that ample time has passed, I realized if only I had taken the time to read through her answers, I would have seen that her favorite song was Lou Reed's "Walk on the Wild Side"; how often she wrote *kinky, mind-blowing* and *gender-bending* to describe her daily activities.

Do not make the same mistake!

■ ■ ■

Do: Be ready to stare at your iPhone when they say: *Messaging makes talking obsolete.*

■ ■ ■

Do: Wonder. If they marked: *We both Speak English…*why they wrote their essay in French?

■ ■ ■

Do: Remind yourself while they checked: *We Both Like Rock and Roll;* they added…*it's the devils music.*

■ ■ ■

Do: Question their empathy when they said: *If you want breakfast in bed, you should go live in a hotel.*

■ ■ ■

Don't: Check *Intimate Conversation* until you learn if they are hearing-impaired.

■ ■ ■

Don't: Be quick to anger. You deserve to be called *nasty* when you write: *I love naughty limericks.*

■ ■ ■

Don't: Be judgmental. For some, *Classic Comics* are the equal to *Melville, Dickens, and Gabriel García Márquez.*

■ ■ ■

Don't: Request a do-over if only get one answer right. Remember, *"One" is the loneliest number for a reason...*

■ ■ ■

Don't: Think he's *got low T if he says: he loves sitting around the fire at night, with a glass of wine in his hand, talking about the Meaning of Life.*

■ ■ ■

Don't: Jump to conclusions. OK, he's white as a ghost, but find out what sunscreen he uses. Maybe he does take long walks on a sunlit beach.

■ ■ ■

Don't: Take her literally. When she says: *a woman's asking for it if she gets into a car with tinted windows,* she's probably not talking about your *Fiat.*

■ ■ ■

Don't: Think she's going to go see *The Chronicles of Riddick,* when she says, *unless she sees nuns coming out of the film singing, she won't buy a ticket.*

■ ■ ■

Don't: Be hypocritical. If you went overboard and checked: *artistic, romantic, humorous, witty, friendly, kind, spiritual, and self-confident*—why can't he?

■ ■ ■

Don't: Think you're going to have an open and honest relationship when they write: *when it comes to plastic surgery, their policy is: "Don't ask, don't tell."*

■ ■ ■

Absolutely Do Not: Forget who you are. Sure it's hard if he likes barbecue and looks like Clint Eastwood, but you're a Vegan—stay strong!

■　■　■

I'm looking for someone adorable to adore and have no idea how any psychological test can help me in that area.
Linda, sixties, widow

■　■　■

I don't think I want to meet you based on many difference in likes and dislikes, but I wanted you to know that what you wrote is hysterical.
Beth, fifties, single

■　■　■

Am looking for compatible, petite, honest woman for long-term relationship and was able to get my answers from this section. So far, while no instantaneous chemistry, the women I've met were honest in their answers and made every date enjoyable.
Jack, fifty-nine, widower

■　■　■

I think I've finally found Mr. Sensitive when he tells me he loved Chick Flicks. When I asked if he liked "Beaches" he goes all happy on me, says it's one of his favorite film, and to prove it, shows me all his Chick Flicks on his "Netflix" cue. Only, instead of "Beaches," I see "Bitches on the Beach." Instead of "Sweet November" it's "Sweet Cheeks Cheri." And "Bed of Roses"...I'm too embarrassed to repeat that one!
Helen, fifties, divorced

■　■　■

Nothing bothers me more than two people sitting across from each other staring down at their phones. Now, I'm not a crazy person about it, but if I have an opportunity, I make it a point to mention this very clearly in my profile and in the first contact I have with any gentlemen who contacts me. It never occurred to me I'd be OK with him getting up from the table every five minutes to answer his cell. I mean, what do I have to do, spell it out?"
Ellyn, late fifties, divorced

■ ■ ■

I think you can take honesty up to a point. I have one friend who is on anxiety meds, and I told her there is no reason to mention it. It will only scare off guys because they'll think you're a nervous wreck. Another friend has osteoporosis, however, you can't tell it by looking at her. I told her men will immediately think she's a cripple. I've had fights with them, and we end up not talking to each other for days. They think I'm the bad one here. I'm just using common sense, that's all...
GGG, sixty-five, widow

■ ■ ■

Your Reply and What You Should Say

■ ■ ■

The odd thing about this form of communication is
that you're more likely to talk about nothing than something.
But I just want to say that all this nothing
has meant more to me than so many somethings.

—KATHLEEN TO JOE, *YOU'VE GOT MAIL*

REMEMBER WHAT I said about receiving my first message? How I wanted to chest bump with the wall? That wasn't the worst of it. After realizing there was someone out there who liked me, it occurred it might be a good opportunity to propose marriage, or at least, a hint as to where I'd like to honeymoon.

I'm just kidding. Well, actually, those thoughts did cross my mind, but you can see where I'm going.

Cooler heads did prevail, and I sent out a message that was short and sweet, making sure to thank her for the e-mail, complimenting her on her profile, and finally suggesting a time we could talk on the phone.

When I broached this subject with dating vets, they all had similar experiences, although one or two became so excited and so overwhelmed, they lost control with tragic results.

Take the story of this online vet who, earlier that morning, had the opportunity to pass a celebrity on the street. Not just any celebrity, but one of this woman's favorite movie heroines. Thinking this a wonderful omen, when she received her first message, decided to give the poor fellow, who was only looking to start a conversation, the story of how with a stalker's maniacal stealth and persistence, she followed let's say—Julia

317

Roberts—from block to block, store to store until the star finally slipped into her apartment building.

While not as smarmy as the online vet who replied: *My hotel or yours;* or as sexually charged as the woman who wrote *a haiku to the man's six-pack-abs*—it's enough you're sending your first message into cyberspace without *wandering into never-never-land with Julia Roberts.*

■　■　■

Do: Remember men *have selective memories.* So—*amiable* or *agreeable* will be only taken out of context to mean, *you're one easy piece.*

■　■　■

Don't: Sign *your humble servant* unless you intend to be one.

■　■　■

Don't: Pledge to mail yourself *COD* if you like to take things slow.

■　■　■

Don't: Add *Cc or Bcc,* or they'll think you're a *groupie or a gossip.*

■　■　■

Don't: Be a hypocrite and include *Bible quotes* on a site for *agnostics.*

■　■　■

Don't: Promise you'll leave the light on for them unless you want a *quickie.*

■　■　■

Don't: Declare you come with *frequent flyer miles* if he has a *fear of flying*.

■ ■ ■

Don't: Guarantee *to send a car* unless you want to *send him home the same way*.

■ ■ ■

Don't: Accuse them of being slowwitted by asking: *What the hell took you so long?*

■ ■ ■

Don't: Overplay the *humility card* and confess: *You can't believe somebody so handsome, would contact somebody so ordinary.*

■ ■ ■

Don't: Go overboard and write: *You're not him! OMG, OMG, OMG! Richard Gere!*

■ ■ ■

Don't: Be surprised he brings a suitcase when you include a *video tour of your eightieth floor penthouse.*

■ ■ ■

Don't: Oversell and add…you come with: *Amazon Advantage, Groupon promo codes,* or the aforementioned, *frequent flyer miles.*

■ ■ ■

Don't: Declare *God must have been listening when he sent you to me* when you're on a site for atheists.

■ ■ ■

Don't: Supply a video of you and two girlfriends romping around at a pajama party when his screen name is, *ShyGuy111.*

■ ■ ■

Absolutely Do Not: Cut and paste your response *without changing his first name.* (Do I need to remind you, if you cut and paste, *never use Cc or Bcc.)*

■ ■ ■

It's a crapshoot. I just try to be honest and hope for the best.
Helen, fifties, divorced

■ ■ ■

Today two wonderful things happened. I received your message and I picked up my 2017 Corvette Stingray! What are you doing this Saturday afternoon?
Mel, fifties, divorced twice

■ ■ ■

Loved your message, your profile. So amusing. You ignited a spark in me. Must tell you I walked across France last April and now contemplating my next adventure. Perhaps England…perhaps with you? Isn't that a lovely thought? Love to connect. Talk. Skype? Whatever?
Gloria, fifty-five, widow

■ ■ ■

Said my age was seventy-two. Wrote not dead, plenty of life and looking for someone with equal parts moxie and muster. OK, age requirements were forty to fifty but no reason for replies like: "Might as well be!" "Water seeks its own level." And "Who uses words like moxie *and* muster?"
Gavin, seventy-two, widower

■ ■ ■

I find you and your profile intriguing. In the interest of being totally honest, I will likely be unavailable to meet with you until mid-February in order to recover from an injury. However, looking forward to communicating via e-mail. You appear to be a kind and understanding woman. I hope you are.
Harry, eighties, widower

■ ■ ■

Dear Delicious Orchard Man: Has anyone told you look like Gene Wilder? I'm no Gilda Radner-lookalike but I do have a great sense of humor. Since we both are organic gardeners and live in rural communities, you in Connecticut, me in Long Island, I think we have common soil from which to grow a serious relationship. Write me. PS love your screen name. Wish mine were as clever.
Name withheld (wrote to Steve, sixties, divorced)

■ ■ ■

You said the most important part of a relationship is being real and in the moment. I hope so too and look forward to meeting you, taking a long walk perhaps and showing how willing I am to be open to developing a trust that enables us to share our vulnerable sides. If this is something worth exploring and if my picture lights your fire, I'm your guy. Have car so coming out to your neck of the woods isn't a problem. Are you game?
Jack, fifty-nine, widower

■ ■ ■

I loved what you said about age…how old would you be if you didn't know how old you were…I don't know if that was an original quote or not but it made me want to write you back ASAP. I was also happy to see that you share my desire to meet someone who is somewhat independent yet eager to be together and still sees life as an adventure.

Burt, seventy-eight, widower

■　■　■

Instead of me telling you about what you should reply, how about if I tell you how important it is to know who you are replying to! How about me telling you about the absolute worst first date any woman can have. I meet a guy online and we get together for coffee. As soon as I sit down I know it's not going to work so, I try to drink it as fast as I can, nearly scalding my throat in the process. I wasn't going to throw it out, cost a lot of money. By the way, I always pay for my own coffee. So I'm done with him but I let him off gently. Hold it if you think this is the last of it, I assure you it's not. I meet another guy who I like. We agree to meet at a park, but something comes up. I think a friend got sick so, I was distracted, really couldn't keep the date. Well, I look for his number but can't find it and end up standing him up and I'm feeling really bad. Two or three weeks later I'm cleaning out my bag and I find his number. I call and tell him I'm sorry I stood him up. He's not mad, says he's so glad I called, because he's been thinking about me. We say we're going to meet at a bar, have a drink and hang out. I get there early, waiting for my date and who walks in but the loser I blew off several weeks ago? I figure he's also there to meet someone from the Internet. He comes over, we exchange hellos and then to get rid of him, because my guy's about to show, I say something like nice seeing you but I'm sure you have to go and he says no, sits down and says he's happy I called him again. All of a sudden I say to myself, ahh shit, I contacted the wrong guy and now I have to dump him again! I had to make up some story. Told him although I had powerful feelings toward him and that's why I called again, now that's he's here I realized I can't get involved in any intense relationship, because my mother's sick and one of my dogs is dying. So here's the rule. Keep your men straight when they have the same name. Make some note to where

they live, characteristic that distinguishes them, otherwise, you'll get confused, embarrassed and have to make up some stupid shit."
Helen, fifties, divorced

■　■　■

Option Two: You Make the First Move

■ ■ ■

The heart wants what the heart wants.

—WOODY ALLEN

HOLD ONTO YOUR hats! While their profiles are stirring up your hormones, *your profile* is working the same magic on them and your mailbox should be filling up with invitations to the Big Dance!

Now, I know what you're thinking. How can I handle this embarrassment of riches? Easy-peasy. *You prioritized.*

If you're the kind of gal who likes to be pursued, pour yourself a glass of vino and cautiously open each message, one at a time. When you're finished jumping around the living room singing "Celebration," follow my *Dos* and *Don'ts* and see where the cookie crumbles.

If you like to be the *pursuer,* just lick your lips, assume the familiar lean and hungry pose and go to it. As one of my female friends describes the process: *"Think of it as an all-you-can-eat buffet where you can fill up to your heart's content without gaining a pound, growing an inch, or throwing up."*

Guys fall into the same passive-aggressive categories, so my advice to you is also *prioritizing.*

I also advise you to *get over yourselves.* Unlike some of my online vets who became so emboldened by an embarrassment of riches and thought they were God's Gift to women, you must avoid becoming so full of yourself, you turn off every women with messages like: *This is your lucky day! I'm going to rock your world! Make sure you like to travel, cause I'm gonna send you to heaven!*

In the interest of keeping this clean, I've omitted their naughty limericks and boastful guarantees of sexual nirvana.

(Warning! Remember, until you know they're looking to steal your love and not your identity, NO PERSONAL INFO, NO WAY, NO HOW.)

■ ■ ■

I always try to put myself in his place, figure out what he wants me to say. Sure, I'm always second-guessing myself…what can I say?
GGG, sixty-five, widow

■ ■ ■

"I am that person who can make someone very happy." Women like it when you put them before you. Not that I don't mean it, but you have to use a little psychology.
Steve, sixties, divorced

■ ■ ■

I realized I was thinking of you, and I began to wonder how long you'd been on my mind. Then it occurred to me: Since I've seen your profile, you've never left. Write me.
Laura, late sixties, widow

■ ■ ■

I want to meet someone who is warm, active, intelligent, cheerful, physically fit, playful, romantic, somewhat independent yet eager to be together, and still sees life as an adventure. You seem to fit the bill.
Terry, seventies, divorced

■ ■ ■

Love your humor, but I do wear Manolos and Louboutins, but then again I was a shoe designer and wear to appropriate places of course!
LG, early sixties

. . .

When I saw his profile, I contacted him. Did it with what they call a "wink." It's where you choose a short statement. I said, "your profile made me smile..." He responded, sent me questions, and the rest is history.
Beth, fifty, single

. . .

I am a PhD. I am handsome, athletic, very bright, very sensuous, romantic, caring, street smart, can listen well, and carry on a conversation, all the traits listed in your profile. Ergo, a perfect match with you!
LC, fifties, single

. . .

Your profile brought tears to my eyes—laughing of course! You seem delightful, attractive, very smart, fun, and most important, real...I too am real, what you see is what you get, so let's check each other out more closely.
I look forward to hearing from you.
Donna, sixty-eight, divorced

. . .

My secret? How come I'm nearly sure my first date won't be a complete bust? I never e-mail anyone unless they've already e-mailed me. Gives me a chance to check 'em out. Make sure I like their looks. They don't write anything that makes them look like a jerk. Especially misspelled words. Hate that. I even talk to my girlfriends, see if they know the guy. Then I send them a message. Like

I said, not 100 percent guaranteed, but I know I'm the one to reject 'em, not the other-way-round.
Helen, fifties, divorced

■   ■   ■

What Your Message Should Say

■ ■ ■

Do nothing in haste, look well to each step,
and from the beginning what may be the end.

—EDWARD WHYMPER

BEFORE YOU READ this, go back and review the section, *Your Reply and What You Should Say.*

The *Julia Roberts tale* comes to mind and should serve as a warning to what can happen if you don't keep it short and sweet and instead, wander off message.

Speaking of short and sweet, I remember one online vet bragging she never failed to get a response when she simply wrote: *Thinking of you. Hugs.*

I thought that a lovely story, until she added: *Of course, my picture's hot.*

To all you Shallow Hals who prize her picture above all else, don't think just by glorifying her beauty, as one of my interviewers did, there won't be serious blowback.

At first, his gushing adoration did the trick and immediately rewarded him a first date. Unfortunately, when she failed to live up to the image he created with his own words, upon seeing the sadness in his eyes, she began to cry.

He later admitted, she wasn't so terrible-looking, but because he was so consumed by his own bullshit (his words), he was ultimately hoisted by his own petard. (Again, his words)

Oh—and no unsuccessful pickup lines: *Are you good with a whip* never worked before, so don't think it will work for you here, either.

■ ■ ■

328

Do: Limit the e-mails and phone calls to three unless one of you is serving a *life sentence with no hope of parole.*

■　■　■

Do: Think. Unless you're the second coming of *Elizabeth Barrett Browning, dump the poetry and stick to prose.*

■　■　■

Do: Save how you really feel until you meet him *face to face,* and then you can declare: *Yield to your Queen.*

■　■　■

Do: Begin with a question. How else will you know if he likes the *Dirty Harry movies* unless you ask: *Do you feel lucky, punk?*

■　■　■

Do: Ask for *proof of life.* You need to get their *phone number, hear their voice, and prove it's not a mental-health worker writing his or her e-mails.*

■　■　■

Do: Remember: *Men come from Mars and woman from Venus,* so to start a meaningful relationship, just come out and ask: *Your spaceship or mine?*

■　■　■

Don't: Think it's a compliment to ask: *Who's your plastic surgeon?*

■　■　■

Don't: Use *Hot Stuff,* because he might associate it with *Global Warming.*

■ ■ ■

Don't: Ask them to make a decision by writing: *If you want it, come and get it.*

■ ■ ■

Don't: Overdo the humble bit with: *Can this be happening to poor, little ole' me?*

■ ■ ■

Don't: Use clichés. *"You're the answer to all my dreams," will not get an answer.*

■ ■ ■

Don't: Write your own poetry, that is, *I could lick you up and down till you say stop.*

■ ■ ■

Don't: Say *you just won the lottery and your prize is me!* Remember who you are and leave the bullshit to him.

■ ■ ■

Don't: Be totally honest. It's OK to say you find him attractive, but don't confess: *He's so hot you had to take a cold shower just to catch your breath!*

■ ■ ■

Absolutely Do Not: Ruin one of the best movie lines by paraphrasing: *"Of all the women, on all the dating sites, in all the world, you pick me."*

■ ■ ■

Judging your book by its cover, I'd love to curl up and read the rest.
JJ, midseventies, widow

■ ■ ■

My first message? "Thinking of you. Hugs." That always works. Of course, my picture's hot.
CP, fifty, divorced

■ ■ ■

BTW, please do not correct my spelling and return this to me. Run on sentences, use of capitals, and runaway thoughts are my specialty. My pet peeve, there appears to be no spell-check. If you like the "rest of me," meet me halfway and e-mail me.
Ellyn, late fifties, divorced

■ ■ ■

Now...I would love to know a little more about you with a personal note if you would like to consider meeting a very lovely lady "who does look like" her picture. I do live out of the city but come into NY regularly. Just give me ample notice, and we can meet in your favorite bistro.
Linda, sixties, widow

■ ■ ■

A Dream Boat! That's what you are. If your other attributes are as great as your wit, then you are my dream come true. You may hate my profile, but if you get it, please contact me, or else I will be miserable the rest of my life!
GGG, sixty-five, widow

■　■　■

Oh yes, while now far too old to compete in a beauty contest, if you're able to enjoy a reasonably attractive face across the table, I find your photo just that. Hoping to hear your voice as I find that medium to be more revealing.
Nan, fifty-nine, divorced

■　■　■

To know me is to like me. A retired teacher who has returned to my earlier passion, oils. Recently lost a remarkable man I connected with on this site and hopeful the magic repeats. As I grow older, I continue to love learning and exploring new ideas with people as devoted to personal growth as I.
Terry, seventies, divorced

■　■　■

I don't know if it's them or me, but somehow I'm always getting it wrong. I write a very complimentary message. One or two paragraphs, nothing excessive, and I get a response that I'm too wordy. I write a line or two, make sure I'm complimentary and get my message across, and I'm accused of being flip. I just can't seem to get it right. Thought about calling but get a little tongue-tied. And I've been told I have a heavy Brooklyn accent that turns women off.
Gavin, seventy-two, widower

■　■　■

The First Date

■ ■ ■

Some souls just understand each other upon meeting

—N.R. Hart

REMEMBER YOUR FIRST date? Remember what your beau looked like? Doesn't matter, whether you were nine or nineteen, I bet you do. I'll also wager you recall every detail, because it was a moment that promised the thrill of unbridled romance.

When your date came to the door, I'll also bet any apprehension vanished, as his youthful gaze shone upon you, and made you glow from head to toe.

Ladies—try and be that young girl again. Try and recapture those emotions when in the coming days you meet your 100 percent match at the local Starbucks.

What, you don't believe me? You think I'm leading you on, *well you haven't been paying attention to the subtext!* This book is all about putting a little love in your heart—and ladies—you are this close...*So let's party like it's 1984!* (Thanks again, Prince.)

Guys—guys—if you can stop lying to yourself about how many women you seduced before the age of consent, try and honestly recall how you felt when you rang the doorbell that very first time and waited, sucking hard on that Sen-Sen breath mint, for her to open the door.

I remember. I remember, as soon as she opened the door, this huge monster pulled her aside and dragged me in by the lapels of my school blazer. Her Daddy Dearest ripped it so badly, my mom cried for hours as she tried to repair it.

Men—I'm sorry! I'm ruining this for you! I just finished cheering on the ladies, and now I've burdened you with my teenage traumas that continue to prey on me as I fill out this profile.

Come on, even if they still lived with their fathers, the old geezer would be over hundred and couldn't possibly brutalize me again—right?

■   ■   ■

Do: Check 'em out, but hide the *binoculars* when you do decide to come in.

■   ■   ■

Do: Employ a *double if you're a worrier; that way he can't follow you home.*

■   ■   ■

Do: Choose *a motel.* If he doesn't send you *to the ice machine, you've got a keeper.*

■   ■   ■

Do: Bring a mirror. Unless you're meeting at *The Big Apple Circus,* make sure you didn't apply lipstick with the back of your hand.

■   ■   ■

Don't: Pick a place that requires steep steps unless you're ready to administer CPR.

■   ■   ■

Don't: Wait until you're too smitten to speak. Just come right out and ask if it's a *fever blister.*

■   ■   ■

Don't: Hold his photo to his balding dome and ask another customer: *Do you see my problem?*

■   ■   ■

Don't: Come an *hour late*. There're other ways to test how much *they want to have a relationship.*

■   ■   ■

Don't: Throw *stones at glass houses*. Yanking his *hairpiece* off could cause him to grab your *implants*.

■   ■   ■

Don't: Bring a *Wedding Planner*. He could have had his fingers crossed when he made those promises.

■   ■   ■

Don't: Pick a place you've used before. They're not going to like it when you walk in, and half the patrons either *wave or boo*.

■   ■   ■

Don't: Come with anything larger than a *small purse*. He'll think you want to move in or leave town to get away from him.

■   ■   ■

Don't: Split his lip if *he wants to split the check*. Just gently remind him of your *Black Belt*. (And, I don't mean *Gucci*.)

■   ■   ■

Don't: Toss the *sugar packet* to see if they've still got their *reflexes*. You'll *miss and injure someone at another table.*

■　■　■

Don't: Take *muscle relaxers.* He'll mistake the skeletal collapse for boredom and stop talking about taking you for a cruise.

■　■　■

Don't: Hide your insecurities about your memory. If you think you've already dated the guy, just ask if it's his turn to pay.

■　■　■

Don't: Jump the gun (again) and (this time) wear a *wedding dress.* It'll only make him feel he should have at least worn a jacket.

■　■　■

Don't: Select anything with *caramel.* They'll confuse your inability to speak as proof they're worthless, not the fault of your implants.

■　■　■

Don't: Let anything distract you, even their *Caramel Waffle Cone Crème Frappuccino Blended Crème* you can't take your eyes off.

■　■　■

Absolutely Do Not: Ask if *that's a banana in his pants when* you're *wearing the high-rise booty bra* and *bubble buns boyshorts panty.*

■　■　■

I'm hoping for the best but preparing for the worse so I'm never disappointed.
FC, fifty-nine, divorced

■ ■ ■

Always give him the option of picking the place. Best way to find out if he's cheap or not.
CP, fifties, divorced

■ ■ ■

Nothing is perfect! It's the imperfections that make life interesting. A glass of wine, good conversation, and a laugh is a good place to start.
Chris, sixty-seven, divorced

■ ■ ■

I understand at my age I'm setting myself up for disappointment, but I can't help it. I think this next one's going to make me his bride.
Shirl, seventy, divorced

■ ■ ■

I knew within five minutes he wasn't for me, but he felt the opposite. He said as soon as he saw me he knew I was the one. When I just shook my head, he said his late wife said the same, but just like her, we were going to live happily ever after. I said we aren't even going to finish this drink together. So I left.
Laura, late sixties, widow

■ ■ ■

There was a guy who asked to come upstairs to use the loo. It was my fault, breaking my own rules for never letting a first date learn where you live, or letting him into my apartment. He had a long train ride ahead of him and

needed to pee. Then he has the nerve to look at his watch, say he'll have to wait two hours for the next train and wonders if he could sleep over in the extra bedroom, when he knows I live in a studio. What kills me is, I didn't pay attention to the warning signs. Who talks about penile implants?
Linda, sixties, widow

■　■　■

So I meet a gentleman on a dating website, and he doesn't seem like a mass murderer, and after a phone conversation, we agree to meet. We had a nice coffee date, and he asks me out for dinner. I didn't think it was going anyplace, but I agreed. The restaurant was out in Smith Town, and I took my car, because I didn't want to be stuck there if it didn't turn out to my liking and I wanted to leave. Now, this was before GPS, so I'm driving along, trying to find my way in an industrial area with oil tanks and, in my head, I'm thinking I have no idea where I am going. I have my doors locked, and I'm about to give up and go home when I see lights up ahead. It's a little Italian restaurant and looked like it's a scene right out of "The Godfather." I park my car, go inside, and it's very clear I'm the only Jewish person in the whole place. The maître di found me and brought me over to the guy. I sat down, and we ordered dinner and wine, and the man tells me how much he enjoyed meeting me, how much he'd like to date me and have me as his girlfriend, but he wanted to be completely honest with me and proceeded to tell me about the house he lived in and how it had ghosts. So already I thought he was a little strange. Then he goes on to tell me he's been away for a while. Stupid me, I think he's been on vacation, but then he says, "but the Feds never found the money." I didn't want to cause any problems, so I tried my best to be cordial; however, I made it clear we weren't a match. I thought he took it well; I mean he let me leave. I went home, and at that time my mom was living with me, so I say, guess what mommy, I just had a date with the mob.
Helen, fifties, divorced

■　■　■

In Conclusion

■ ■ ■

You can't be beaten by something you laugh at.

—JONATHAN HARNISCH

WELL—LADIES AND Germs (forgive me, sometimes I still think I'm seven), I'm sorry to bid you so long and farewell, but now the real fun is about to begin. Rest assured, you've got the best out of me, and you're ready to rock and roll.

I'm convinced that after reading this book, when you log in and glance over the questions, you will not run from the room screaming: *I'd rather be alone and miserable for the rest of my life than put myself through this shit!*

Instead, I'm sure it will remind you of when, in seventh grade, you scanned the history questions and said to yourself: *Mr. Morris' so lazy, he's gonna give you the same test he gave last week!*

Not only will you relive that youthful feeling but also you'll *look young again, too.* I'll make sure of that when you post your photos, a selection so photogenic, they'll be sure to knock *ten years off your age,* as well as, *knock their socks off.*

When you come to the essay, you'll follow my advice and pen one so full of wit and wisdom, you'll send it off to the *New Yorker;* and they will eagerly share it will all their readers, it's so damn good.

When you complete the last category, and review all your answers, you'll toast yourself for a job well done, and say to yourself: *If they don't see how perfectly perfect I am, well f-'em and the horse they rode in on.*

Finally, when you meet your date at a time and place of your choice, you'll be in command, deciding with one motion of the hand, whether they sit and share with you a *Caramel Waffle Cone Crème Frappuccino Blended Crème*, or beat feet.

OK, OK—so I'm exaggerating a little. So this entire book is a little over the top. How else, can I get you to lighten up and laugh at a process that asks you to trust a *math equation to find love and romance in something so unreal as cyberspace?*

It's almost as bizarre as asking Luke Skywalker *to find love in the Chalmun's Cantina without having Yoda to give him a heads-up.*

I hope I've given you a heads-up, as well as a few laughs; prepared you to face this brave new world with a smile on your face, a laugh in your heart, and maybe some giggles.

Oh—and remember the sage words of one online vet who summed up the dating process with these words: *Think of it as an all-you-can-eat buffet where you can fill up to your heart's content without gaining a pound, growing an inch or throwing up.*

■   ■   ■

I'm off it. Decided no free dinner was worth it.
Laura, late sixties, widow

■   ■   ■

I believe in planned spontaneity, and Internet dating fits the bill to a T.
Jack, fifty-nine, widower

■   ■   ■

To be healthy. To be happy. To always have love and empathy in my heart.
Ellyn, late fifties, divorced

■   ■   ■

Made me get out of the house and have a social life again.
Burt, seventy-eight, widower

■ ■ ■

The best advice I can give if he's making unwarranted sexual advances is to mention that you live with your sister who's a nurse and happens to treat patients with sexually transmitted diseases, and would he like to hear some of the stories she told her.
Nan, fifty-nine, divorced

■ ■ ■

Can't believe you haven't had more people tell you they've met someone online. Jackie and I are just one of three couples we know married someone they met there. I think our relationship was the longest, two years after we connected. If I'm not mistaken, the other two couples met and married inside of a year.
Betty, sixty-seven, divorced

■ ■ ■

I was on the checkout line at Trader Joes when a gentleman taps me on the shoulder and asks if we've ever met? I must have shown how frightened I was by my expression because he immediately expressed his apology. Later I thought, well, he's my age, maybe we do know each other? Finally, it dawned on me. We had messaged each other online but for some reason, never connected. I contacted him immediately. We've been dating for three months. I tell this story to my girlfriends when they ask if they should take the plunge and go onto an online dating site.
CP, fifties, divorced

■ ■ ■

I've never told anybody this before, but I sing a little song to myself before I go on the site. It's called, "What I did for love." It worked for me...maybe it'll work for you? Come on, try it now...
Name withheld (told to the Author)

■　■　■

Acknowledgments

Lighten Up and Log In for Love could not have been written without the support and wisdom of the many online veterans who honestly and courageously told me their stories so readers of this book could benefit from their experiences. In particular, I would like to thank Helen and Linda who provided the initial spark; and together with Cheryl, Steve, Karen, Angela, Lucille, Susan, Peter and Sally provided the expertise and friendship that sustained me through the process. I would like to thank Emily@ fiverr.com/Probookcover 258 for the cover design and CreateSpace for the copy editing and for designing the book's interior.

About the Author

Eric Robespierre was born and raised in New York City. He has worked as a screenwriter, playwright, documentary film director and web designer. He has been an award winning advertising copywriter creating campaigns for Mitsubishi, Izod Lacoste, and other major brands.

Robespierre is now a full-time writer. Together with Helen Brand he wrote *The Yummy Hunter's Guide: The Best-Tasting, Low-Calorie Foods and Where to Shop for Them*. He is also the author of *Cracking the Walnut: How Being a Little Nuts Helped Me to Beat Prostate Cancer*, and *Living Large in America: The Life and Times of the Family Ginsburg (Pronounced Du Pont)*.

Visit Eric Robespierre at:
www.ericrobespierre.com

www.ingramcontent.com/pod-product-compliance
Lightning Source LLC
LaVergne TN
LVHW011216080426
835509LV00005B/157